TEACH YOU
SLEEP THROUGH THE NIGHT

TEACH YOUR BABY TO SLEEP THROUGH THE NIGHT

Charles E. Schaefer, Ph.D.

and

Michael R. Petronko, Ph.D.

THORSONS PUBLISHING GROUP

First UK Edition published 1989

First published by G. P. Putnam's Sons,
200 Madison Avenue, New York, NY 10016, USA

British Library Cataloguing in Publication Data

Schaefer, Charles E.
Teach your baby to sleep through the night.
1. Babies. Home care — Manuals
I. Title   II. Petronko, Michael R.
649'.122

ISBN 0-7225-1774-2

*Published by Thorsons Publishers Limited,
Wellingborough, Northamptonshire, NN8 2RQ, England*

Printed in Great Britain by Cox & Wyman Limited,
Reading, Berkshire

3 5 7 9 10 8 6 4 2

To our wives, Anne and Pat

Acknowledgments

Our deepest thanks to Theresa Foy DiGeronimo for helping this book reach its final form.

We also want to thank Judy Linden for her enthusiasm, interest and support throughout all phases of the publishing process.

Contents

Contents

TEACH YOUR BABY TO
SLEEP THROUGH THE NIGHT

1

IS THIS PROGRAM FOR ME?

You are not alone. Every day parents walk through the door of our Crying Baby Clinic looking for some way to make their baby stop crying during the night. These parents are exhausted, nervous, and depressed. Some also feel embarrassed because their pediatrician has laughed off their complaints with a curt, "Babies are supposed to cry." Others feel inadequate because family and friends have pointed an accusing finger at their parenting skills.

Only those of us who have been deprived of sleep over a long period of time can understand its devastating effects. But sleep deprivation is not something that "goes with having a baby." It is a serious physical concern that can lead to disorientation, weight loss, chronic fatigue, irritability, depression, broken marriages and child abuse. Therefore, our goal in working with these parents and in writing this book is threefold. First, we want to assure you that there are many parents just like you suffering through sleepless nights. (Studies have found two-thirds of all babies six to twelve months old and 20–30 percent of all children one to three years old have trouble sleeping through the night.) Second, we want to give you a quick and practical technique that will teach your baby how to sleep through the night without relying on you for help. And third, we want to offer stress-management strategies that will help you cope with the problems connected with raising a crying baby.

Our program for teaching babies to sleep through the night is called the Quick-Check Method. It is a behavioral approach tailored to work for normal, healthy children between the ages of six months and three years. The program is structured to give quick relief from night waking and crying.

We have found that infant sleep problems are usually of two kinds: babies who can't get to sleep without external help, like rocking, walking, feeding, patting, etc.; and babies who continually wake during the night and can't fall back to sleep without this same help. Our program addresses both of these problems.

With our program, most babies can learn to sleep through the night after three nights of training. But as every parent and developmental psychologist knows, each child is different. So, although your baby's training may take longer, you should see a substantial reduction in night crying within one week.

There are, however, a number of reasons why this approach to sleep training may not be for your baby. Our method is not intended, for example, to solve medical problems. It should not be used if your child's sleeplessness stems from physical ailments, such as earaches, teething pain, or neurological disturbances. We recommend that before beginning our program, you ask your pediatrician to rule out the physical ailments listed in chapter 5. Also, if your baby has a combination of sleep problems—such as a difficult personality combined with night terrors, illness, and inconsistent parenting—then we recommend you see a pediatric sleep therapist for a full evaluation before starting our program.

Once you've determined that your baby has no medical reason for his nocturnal wakings, you must then consider the fact that our learn-to-sleep system needs the support of the entire family. The program most often fails in families who argue over the best solution. If one parent supports a program that offers comfort on demand while the other tries to follow the techniques outlined in this book, the baby will be further aggravated by his parents' inconsistency and will not respond positively.

Also, our program requires that you let your baby cry. It helps to remember that we all let out squeals of protest when we're trying to break a bad habit, and so will your baby. (Crying even has some benefits that we'll explain in chapter 2.) It's important for you to believe that by putting up with some crying now, you'll save your baby and yourself a lot of distress later on.

We know that every minute of screaming is its own eternity to an anxious parent, so we have included ways to minimize the stressful elements of our approach. (See chapter 6.) Nevertheless, if you can't tolerate the sound of your baby crying, our program is definitely not for you.

Based on our work with crying babies, we feel that you do your child a disservice by reinforcing bad sleeping habits. Poor sleep patterns make life difficult and confusing for your child. You have taught him to need your help to fall asleep—then you often respond with anger and resentment when he calls for you in the middle of the night. These poor sleep habits are also hard on the whole family. Eventually everyone suffers from fatigue and irritability.

While your baby is an infant, it may seem easier to cater to his need for external help, but it's not in his best interest. To benefit from our program, you must honestly want to help your baby develop a regular sleeping pattern. You must believe that your baby needs your help and guidance to break a bad habit, and you would let him down by giving up when the crying gets too loud. On the first night of sleep training, many of the parents we've worked with have had doubts about the value of independent sleep for their baby. They ask themselves questions like: "What difference does it really make if the baby needs me to help him go to sleep? He needs me for a lot of things during the day, and I never refuse to help him then." Or, "I work all day to meet his needs and make him happy; now at night why should I be selfish and refuse to answer his cries?" And, "Why bother at all? This program was supposed to give us a good night's sleep, but instead we're all wide awake, tense and miserable." These doubts continue to grow through the night because crying is a strong persuader.

That's why it's important to read this entire book before starting the technique with your baby. The information gathered in each chapter will equip you mentally to stand firm until your baby has learned to fall asleep without your help.

Some parents don't mind answering their baby's demands for nocturnal attention. Their life-style is such that it is not an inconvenience for them to rock, walk, or pat the baby to sleep each night. And some parents whose babies wake continually through the night have found an acceptable solution in allowing the baby to sleep in their bed. If you are happy with your baby's nighttime routine, there is no need for sleep training. We certainly do not want to push our philosophy on anyone whose needs do not match our program. You should, however, heed a word of caution. If you think you are willing to put up with restless nights "until he grows out of it," you may be in for a long wait. Once a child has been taught that he cannot fall asleep without his parents' help, it is often years before he can break that habit by himself. A documented study of three-year-old night wakers found that 80 percent of the children were also night wakers at fourteen months old. Obviously it is not advisable to wait for your baby to outgrow this problem. He needs a full night's sleep now, and so do you.

The parents of night wakers often come to us for the sake of their marriage. After several months of disturbed sleep, it is not unusual for the parents of a sleep-disorder child to cancel all evening engagements because they know that a babysitter couldn't get their child to sleep. An occasional vacation alone is also out of the question, and sex becomes a scheduling nightmare. New parents usually don't mind the sacrifice because they believe it's only for a short time. But when months grow into years, the stress can be overwhelming.

Not only do a baby's poor sleep habits limit his parents' social life, rule out any vacations without him, and reduce their opportunities for sex, they also compound a crisis situation. Mike and Tracy had shared their bed with two-year-old Joey since he was born. They had trained him to need their closeness in order to fall asleep. They weren't bothered by the occasional inconvenience it caused until the night Tracy had to rush Mike to the hospital for treatment of a painful kidney stone. While they both spent the night at the hospital, Joey was left in the competent hands of his grandfather. But when he woke up and found his parents missing, he had no independent resources to help him go back to sleep. "That one night made me realize," says Tracy, "that it wasn't good for Joey to be so dependent on us during the night. We had taken away his natural ability to soothe himself back to sleep. It was hard to change his nighttime routine, but I'm sure it's best for him in the long run."

We have written this book for parents like Mike and Tracy who no longer want to reinforce the bad sleeping habits of their children. We have tried to make it enjoyable to read and straight to the point. We have written each page with compassion for your confusion and anxiety and with appreciation for your sincere desire to do what is best for your children.

How do you know if this program is for you? Ask yourself these questions:

1. Has my pediatrician indicated there is no medical reason for my baby's poor sleep patterns?

2. Do I have the support of my entire family?

3. Can I tolerate a few nights of crying?

4. Do I honestly want my baby to learn how to fall asleep without my help?

If you can answer "yes" to these questions, then read on—a good night's sleep is just a few days away!

2

WHY BABIES CRY
AT NIGHT

Babies cry at night for many reasons. They may cry because they have not yet developed a normal sleeping pattern that enables them to sleep for an extended period of time. Sometimes they have not yet established a normal feeding schedule, and so they wake with hunger pains. And they cry because that's what babies do when they want attention. Although there are many other causes of long-term night crying, these three are the most common.

This chapter will give you some general guidelines on normal and abnormal sleeping, crying, and feeding patterns. This information will help you determine if your child's night-crying behavior is typical for his age and experience.

Sleeping Habits

After many years of sleep research, it is still unclear why we need to sleep. It is certain, however, that a person's natural sleep patterns are biologically determined. Just as your baby is born with a unique waking personality, so is he born with a sleep personality. We also know of two kinds of sleep: *quiet sleep*, a deep sleep state characterized by regular respiration, firmly closed eyes, and no eye or body movements; and *active sleep*, a light sleep state characterized by closed eyes with eye movement under the lids, frequent body movement, and irregular respiration patterns.

An adult typically spends 80 percent of his sleep time in quiet deep sleep, and 20 percent in active light sleep. But until an infant is eight or nine months old, he splits his time evenly, with 50 percent of his sleep time spent in each level. During active sleep he is easily awakened by even the creak of a door. No wonder babies are more prone to night waking than adults!

As a baby's quiet sleep time increases, he is more able to sleep for longer periods without being easily awakened. And since some babies cry out as they pass from one level of sleep to another, there are fewer of these transitional cries. It is the growth of quiet sleep time that allows a baby eventually to take on his parents' nighttime sleeping patterns. But if this were *always* the case, you obviously would not be reading this book.

Just as the quality of an infant's sleep changes with age, so does the quantity. It is quite obvious that children require less sleep as they mature through childhood and adolescence. The average newborn sleeps in a series of naps for sixteen to seventeen hours a day. This naplike sleep occurs on and off (usually three hours asleep, one hour awake) throughout each twenty-four-hour period. By sixteen weeks the average infant's sleep requirement is down to fourteen or fifteen hours in three or four more predictable and longer sleeping periods. So infants normally develop a regular sleep/wake rhythm by three to four months of age and will sleep for a consecutive period of nine hours during the night. An infant who has not developed such a pattern by six months and who wakes up more than three nights a week for more than one month is one who has a sleep problem.

Although it would be nice if all babies slept from 8:00 PM to 8:00 AM, the phrase "sleeping through the night" really means sleeping from midnight to 5:00 AM. This means that a baby who is getting his five hours of sleep from 8:00 PM to 2:00 AM may not really have a sleep problem—he may have a scheduling problem.

Sleeping through the night also does not mean that the baby never awakens after midnight. But if the baby does wake (as most do), he should be able to put himself back to sleep without disturbing his parents. As reported in *Psychophysiology* 13 (pp. 155–58), video studies of infants' nighttime sleep habits by T. Anders and A. Sostek have documented that about 80 percent of the twelve-month-old babies studied woke up at night for short periods, but about 60 percent of this group lay quietly in bed and then went back to sleep without making any fuss. This is precisely the goal of sleep training. You want your baby to be able to fall asleep, wake up, and then fall back to sleep without disturbing *your* sleep each time he awakens.

Researchers Moor and Ucko from the University of London Institutes of Education and Child Health wanted to know at what age infants could be expected to sleep through the night. They found that 70 percent of the babies they studied were sleeping through the night by the age of three months, and another 13 percent by the age of six months. They also found that 10 percent never slept through at any time in the first year. And most interestingly, almost 50 percent of those babies who slept through the night before six months reverted to night waking at some time in the second half of the first year. Many of our clients tell us the same story: "He had been sleeping through the night for several months. Then all of a sudden—*bam!*—he's crying out every few hours."

The reason for this reoccurence of night waking after the age of six months (and for the night waking of babies who never learned to sleep through the night) is varied and inexact. Sometimes there is no apparent reason. Other times a baby might sleep fretfully for emotional reasons if his parents are experiencing extreme anxiety or stress. The baby might not sleep well for psychological reasons because he is beginning to suffer separation anxiety or because he is developing a personality that is extremely active or sensitive to external stimulation. And for environmental reasons the baby might change his sleep habits because of changes in his surroundings, such as moving his crib from your room to his own room, or moving to a new home, or simply a change in the room temperature.

Whatever the reason for a baby's night waking, an important factor in our analysis is the parents' response. After six months, a baby quickly learns that a few well-timed cries will bring him attention, cuddling, and other very comforting actions that make it worth his while to wake and cry every night. Then it's time for sleep training! As we will explain in chapter 4, parents can actually teach their babies to be night wakers. One way you can use this information about sleep patterns to help avoid sleep problems is to remember that "sleeping through" is really only a stretch of five hours. Rather than fight with your baby every night at 3:00 AM, for example, maybe you only need to adjust his sleeping schedule. (See Scheduling in chapter 5.) And secondly, you should remember that no one stays in a deep sleep throughout the night. As we go from one level of sleep to another, we all wake and fall back to sleep several times. Babies may cry out when they pass from one stage to another. The anxious parent who rushes in, turns on the light, and picks up the baby is actually destroying the baby's natural ability to fall back to sleep. When your baby cries out in the middle of the night after he's six months old, let him cry for a bit. See if he will eventually soothe himself back to sleep. You'll be surprised how often he will.

Age	Daily Nap Schedule
newborn	7–8 naps a day
4 weeks	4–5 naps a day
16 weeks	3 naps a day (usually separated by 2-hour wakeful periods)
28 weeks	2–3 naps a day—about 2½ hours each
40 weeks	1–2 naps a day (usually a long midmorning nap and an unstable afternoon nap that comes and goes)
1 year	only one nap at midday—about 1½ hours in length (usually from 11:00 AM or 11:30 AM to 12:30 PM or 2:00 PM)
15–18 months	one daily nap following the noon meal (usually lasts for 1½ to 2 hours)
2 years	one nap a day—about one hour in length (it may take longer for the child to drift off to sleep, usually 20 minutes)
3–4 years	many children still take one nap a day, others simply rest, but nap/resttime is still an important time of their day

Naptime: From our analysis of sleep patterns, we find that a baby's night waking is sometimes due to an inappropriate nap schedule. As we mentioned earlier, a newborn's sleep pattern is a continuous series of small naps. But as he matures (at approximately four to six months), his need for daytime sleep can be scheduled so it doesn't interfere with his nighttime sleep. The breakdown of common nap schedules above will help you judge if your night crier is getting too much sleep in the daytime.

Bedtime Routine: From early infancy (three to four months) sleep should be a natural and predictable part of each day. You can help your child adopt this attitude, which might eliminate later bedtime battles, by creating a bedtime and naptime routine.

Set a definite time for sleep once you've established your baby's sleep needs. Let something neutral, like a timer or the clock, signal the sleep time. This eliminates a power struggle.

Make the time before sleep as tranquil as possible. You might sit together and read a book, or you might tell a story or rock your baby and sing a lullaby. Don't roughhouse. If you do play with your baby, play quiet games that will help him unwind. A child who has abnormal sleep habits should not be excited or upset when he goes to bed. If he is, there is very little chance that he will fall asleep without a fight.

Sometimes babies can be calmed before bedtime by being held upright near your left shoulder so they can hear your heart. The sound of a heartbeat will often soothe them. Other babies like rhythmic stimulation and will be calmed down by walking, patting, swinging, rocking, or singing. These are appropriate calming techniques *before* bedtime, but don't try to use them to put your baby to sleep. Doing so would only increase his dependency on you, and you want to be sure your child is always put to bed awake.

Follow a set ritual that lets your baby know sleeptime is approaching, for example, a meal, a bath, a story, and then to bed (or whatever else best fits your schedule). Keep the same sequence of events every night so it is predictable.

Distinguish between bedtime and sleeptime. Most children need fifteen to thirty minutes to settle down before sleep overtakes them. Allow your child to play quietly in his crib or bed if that helps him relax. Sleep will eventually come.

If it takes a tired child over thirty minutes to fall asleep on his own at night and this pattern has continued for over a month, then he has a sleep problem. Many babies with this problem will cry vigorously for an extended period before they fall asleep. The following explanation of crying behavior may help you understand why your child is having difficulty initiating sleep.

Nighttime Crying Patterns

All parents want to know: why do babies cry at night? Unfortunately, the answer is not a simple one. Babies cry at night for different reasons at different ages. The two-month-old who is overstimulated at the end of a busy day cries for a different reason than the eight-month-old who fears separation from his mother. Their cries are different from those of the two-year-old throwing a tantrum, which in turn are completely different from those of the five-year-old who cries because of a bad dream or fear of the dark.

When parents come to our clinic seeking help for their night crier, we begin by analyzing the cry itself. When we learn why the baby is crying, we are better able to decide if sleep training is an appropriate answer to the problem. First it is important to understand that crying in itself is not bad. It is not necessarily evidence of a problem, or a sign of failure on your part. Crying is not always a dilemma that needs a solution or an illness that needs a cure. It is in many ways a positive and healthy sign of development. The cry that signals the birth of a new life is the loud and robust "hello" from a healthy child. As a physical function, this cry serves to speed the transition from fetal circulation to independent pulmonary oxygenation. A newborn's cries are a sign of alertness rather than weakness. Crying generates the heat an infant needs to keep warm. It is also the beginning of his ability to vocalize and his daily aerobic exercise that strengthens his heart and increases his muscular activity. And it is his sole means of releasing tension. These are all reasons why it is *good* for your baby to cry.

Infant crying is natural and even desirable. A newborn cries an average of two and a half hours a day for the first two months for reasons that have nothing to do with the kind of parenting he receives. What a relief for parents to learn that all that crying is not their fault!

Crying also serves as a survival mechanism. A newborn instinctively cries in an aversive and grating manner to assure an immediate response from his parents. This cry is in response to an inborn need. That's why we believe that in the first six months of his life, you cannot spoil a baby by picking him up when he cries. As the infant grows he cries to release tension and to discharge overstimulation. And later his cries become a deliberate effort to communicate. After six months he learns to use his cries as a means of controlling his immediate environment. At this point his night crying may become an unnecessary and inappropriate behavior. When your baby cries out for you in the middle of the night, your response will determine his future sleeping habits. Do you rock him, feed him, or pat his back to put him back to sleep? If so, you may be responsible for teach-

ing him inappropriate sleep associations that will keep him crying out for you all night long. Then it's time to consider sleep
training. You'll have to do some detective work to decide if your
baby is crying to express a real need, such as hunger or pain, or
if he is crying because he has developed poor sleep habits.

Studies have found that parents instinctively react faster to
cries of pain than to cries of boredom. But on a day-to-day basis
most parents find themselves totally baffled by a baby's continuous crying. "I don't know what's wrong with him," say many of
our clients. "He just keeps on crying."

It should be a comfort to know that even trained scientists
who study crying with advanced technological equipment can't
always be sure why a baby is crying. There are, however, some
fairly consistent characteristics of baby cries that will help you
determine the reason why your baby is crying.

Pain Cry

- a sudden onset of loud crying (as opposed to the gradual
  building of other cries)
- an unnaturally long cry (as long as four seconds in con-
  trast to other cries of one second or less)
- an extended period of breath-holding after the initial cry
  (as long as seven seconds)
- a high-pitched cry

Hunger Cry

- a rhythmical cry (cry, pause, cry, pause, etc.)
- a rising and falling melody

· a short cry (one and a half seconds or less)
· a slow, gradual building of volume

(When a hungry baby is left to cry for a long time, the cry will begin to resemble the pain cry.)

Sick Cry

· usually a whiny and nasal tone
· continuous fussing accompanies crying
· A low-intensity cry

Attention Cry

· a whimper at first
· cry builds to a frenzy if not attended to

If you can use the sound of your baby's cry to help determine if he really has a problem that needs your attention, you'll be one step further along in preparing yourself to use our method of sleep training. When it's time to let your baby cry, you'll feel more confident if you can tell he is not sick or in pain.

You can further analyze your baby's night crying by reading chapter 5. When you have eliminated any causes of night crying that are *not* related to poor sleep associations and tried our method for dealing with those that are related to them, you will find that our method is the best way to help your baby learn to sleep through the night.

Another necessary preparatory step is learning how to avoid panicking every time your baby cries. A recent study from the

University of Minnesota supports our belief that crying can be good for babies (and for you too). These researchers discovered there are two kinds of tears. They found that the chemical makeup of physical tears (the kind caused by irritants such as pollen and raw onions) is different from that found in emotional tears (the kind caused by feelings such as sadness). The chemicals found in emotional tears were similar to the physical substances the body makes to fight pain. This explains why we all feel better after having "a good cry." Crying can be healing; it can make your baby feel better. So take a deep breath, relax, and stop feeling guilty and stressed every time your baby cries.

Feeding Schedules

An improper feeding schedule is one of the most common causes of night waking that we encounter at our Crying Baby Clinic. It is easy to fall into the trap of feeding a baby who is not really hungry because this may be the one thing that quiets him. But doing so creates a night crier. Fortunately, parents can quickly resolve this cause of night waking.

At birth babies know exactly how much food they need and how often they need it. They respond to hunger pains with cries for food and they refuse to take more than they need. They generally feed on and off all day and night and sleep in between feedings. Some parents get so accustomed to feeding on demand every few hours that even after the child's digestive system is able to go for longer periods between feedings, they continue to answer all cries with food. This is harmful for the baby in two ways: it disrupts the growth of the child's ability to feel satisfied for at least four hours between feedings and it teaches him to associate food with comfort rather than with hunger.

Sometimes between twelve and sixteen weeks there is a drop-off in a baby's rapid growth rate and, therefore, a decrease in the total number of daily calories he needs. This means he is ready to stop the night feedings. After that time, if your baby's night cries are quieted by a bottle or breast-feeding, it is likely that he is developing poor feeding and sleep habits, and that you are encouraging the problem by providing round-the-clock feeding that he no longer needs. You're also teaching your baby that nighttime, like daytime, is a series of naps followed by feedings. Once he has learned this lesson, he won't stop wanting to be fed during the night until you teach him to sleep without food.

To break this nighttime sleep-eat cycle, you must first help your child adjust to a regular daytime eating schedule. We're always amazed by the parents who bring their night-crying babies to our clinic for sleep training and then immediately give the child a bottle or breast-feeding at the first sign of fussiness. As soon as we see that happen, it's usually easy for us to diagnose the cause of the baby's night waking. Feedings must be given to relieve hunger, not irritability.

Most children from age six months to three years should eat three meals a day with two or three snacks in between. Try to make feeding time fun. Eat something yourself too. This will encourage your baby to eat more at mealtime. Allow twenty to thirty minutes for each meal, but if your child is not eating after that time, remove the food and wait until the next feeding to offer more. Keep the intervals between feedings to three and a half hours or more. If you feed him inconsistently all day, he won't be able to tolerate the long nighttime period without food.

Frequent snacking sets the stage for night-waking hunger pains. If your child becomes fussy before it's time to eat during the day, let him fuss a little—he may just be letting off steam. If he continues being cranky, offer him a pacifier, water, or extra attention and hugs. But don't answer all cries with food.

It is also important to monitor your baby's milk intake. Babies who still take nighttime bottles after they're six months old, may suffer nutritional deficiencies because they are substituting milk for well-balanced meals. From six to twelve months, consider limiting your baby's milk intake to thirty ounces per day. Keep in mind that solids should be 50 percent of their daily calories. From twelve to twenty-four months, limit his milk intake to 24 ounces per day. When you're establishing a daytime feeding schedule, don't let your baby continually cling to the bottle or breast. Try serving his milk or juice in a cup. (The kind with nozzle caps are best for babies who spill.) This is the first step in weaning your baby from the bottle or breast dependency that can be at the root of his night waking.

Next, it's time to begin weaning your baby from the nighttime feedings. By establishing the daytime eating schedule, you will have trained his digestive system to wait for food. If your baby is taking six or more ounces of milk at night, it's not a good idea to just stop the night feedings. A method of gradual weaning is explained in chapter 4, Complications. But if your baby is only taking an ounce or two of milk at each night feeding, try eliminating the feeding completely.

Another reason a child's sleep can be disturbed by feeding problems is an allergy to cow's milk. One study of children less than a year old with a history of both sleep and allergy problems found that when cow's milk was removed from the diet, sleep increased from four and a half hours per night to ten. To prevent an allergic reaction, some nursing mothers limit their intake of whole milk, eggs and peanuts. Check with your doctor if your night waker shows symptoms such as diarrhea, skin rashes, flushed color, or gas after food intake.

Night crying is not always a question of what's normal or abnormal. It's more a matter of deciding what is best for you and your baby. If his night waking is distressful to you and if it is destroying your ability to be a cheerful and loving parent, then it's time for sleep training. Our Quick-Check Method can often provide the solution to the nighttime problems of children who cry too much, sleep too little, and eat too often.

3

WHAT NIGHT CRYING DOES TO YOU

"The day I learned I was pregnant, my husband and I were very excited. Everyone we knew was excited for us too, and many jokingly asked if we were ready for the 'two o'clock feedings.' We laughed, thinking, 'What's so hard about one feeding a night?' Well, twenty months and another child later, we are still waiting for just *one* feeding a night. My daughter, at twenty months old, and my son, at eight months old, have us up four to five times every night. We are all exhausted. During the day we can barely stay awake, and our evenings are a disaster. Our entire night life consists of getting our children to sleep and heading to bed ourselves as quickly as possible to catch a few minutes of sleep before the first one starts crying."

Liane wrote this note to us when she realized that her babies' night wakings were affecting her physical and mental well-being as well as her relationships with her husband, her children and her friends. She and her husband had endured the physical and emotional torment of parenting a night crier for almost two years. Now she wanted to teach her children normal sleep

35

habits so she could once again have some time to herself and time for her husband.

Although there are a number of research studies on the effects of night waking on parents, we have decided not to recount their statistical findings in this chapter. Instead the information we want to pass along to you comes from other parents. The quotations in this chapter illustrating the effects of night crying are taken from the registration form that is completed by each parent who comes to our Crying Baby Clinic. Some quotations are complete and direct ones, others are composites of recurrent complaints. All of them reflect the voices of parents sympathetic to your plight, who realized that night crying was robbing them of the joy of parenthood. They are reaching out to convince you that the vague sense of misery you feel each morning after a bad night with your baby is slowly doing damage to all aspects of your life. Sleep training is not something that parents do because it sounds like a good idea; it is something they *must* do for the sake of their entire family.

Physical Effects

Some of the physical effects of parenting a night crier are obvious: fatigue; red, sore eyes; anxiety; depression; and total exhaustion. One mother wrote us, "Either I'm getting weaker or the baby is getting heavier because lately when he begins his nighttime crying routine, I can barely lug him into my room." This mother is obviously starting to wear down physically. But the increasing weight of her baby is only the beginning of the heavy burden she will carry if her baby continues to disturb her sleep.

Sleep deprivation is so debilitating that it has been used in prison camps and in cult programming to destroy the ability to think and concentrate. Any parent of a night crier can vouch for its effectiveness. "After several months without a good night's sleep," wrote one parent, "my brain has turned into mashed bananas. I can't concentrate long enough to carry on any kind of adult conversation—never mind go back to work!"

Some parents are confused by their chronic exhaustion. "I don't think I should be this tired," wrote Joan. "Even though I get up with the baby three times every night, I still get about seven hours of sleep. Isn't that enough?" That probably would be enough if it were seven consecutive hours. Adding up a few hours here and there, however, will never equal a good night's sleep. In fact, researchers who have studied the effects of light and deep sleeptime on our feeling of well-being believe that four hours of straight, sound sleep will make you feel more rested than seven hours of constantly interrupted sleep.

Night crying is also an intense stress trigger. The cry of an infant is one of the loudest sounds a human being can make. It is equivalent to the sound made by an unmufflered truck in your living room! It's no wonder it makes your heartbeat quicken, your head pound, and your breathing become short and shallow. But in the long term, this stress can have other, more serious and far-reaching consequences. The physical ailments—from ulcers to diabetes—which can be caused by the stress of a night crier are listed in chapter 6. The bottom line, however, was very clearly stated by Claire, when she said to us without a hint of humor in her voice, "This getting up three and four times every night is killing me."

Emotional Effects

"I wanted to be a good mother. I wanted to love my baby with all my heart. I dreamed of days spent reading story books, picnicking in the park and pushing a baby carriage around at the zoo. But now that the baby is here, everything is so different. Since I haven't slept in eleven months, I'm too irritable to play anything with my daughter. I'm too depressed to get dressed in the morning, never mind pack for a picnic. And I'm too tired to even think about walking around at the zoo. Sometimes I'm not even sure if I love my own baby." This battle between the fantasy of being a good parent and the reality of living with a night crier is a common cause of anger and resentment. It's perfectly natural to be angry with someone who takes from you the basic right of sleep. But when that someone is your baby, you begin to juggle the anger and resentment with guilt. The fantasy parent would remain calm, patient and sympathetic to the cries of the child. But you, who are stuck in reality, become short-tempered and cranky. The negative effects of your baby's night waking on your emotional well-being are profound.

You can ease the strain by accepting the reality that parenting is a difficult and tiring job even under the best of circumstances. You can give yourself permission to be irritable and angry. You can also laugh, knowing that because of prolonged sleep deprivation, there is at least one other parent in this world who probably feels like you do. She told us, "Right now I'm not much above the emotional maturity level of my own baby!"

Social Effects

"My brother is getting married in two weeks. All I've done is worry about what will happen when the baby wakes up every two hours that night if I'm not there. I bought a beautiful dress, and I know it should be a nice evening out with my husband. But, instead, I'm a prisoner to my own worries. If I had a choice, I just wouldn't go."

Sue's feelings are echoed every day by the parents we meet at our clinic. These parents tell us that they have given up their social life for three basic reasons:

- "We're just too exhausted even to think of having a good time."
- "We don't want to miss an opportunity to sleep, because we know we'll be up most of the night when we get back."
- "It's impossible to get a babysitter who can stand the constant crying."

Well-intentioned friends tell these parents, "You can't let the baby tie you down so much. Why don't you come out with us next Friday night?" Only another parent of a night crier fully understands why the answer will be, "No, we can't."

Relationships that Suffer

You are different things to different people. You are your child's parent, your spouse's mate, your boss's employee, your mother's child, and your own best friend. All of these relationships are affected by the strain of parenting a night crier. The damaged relationships most commonly mentioned by parents are listed below. If you look closely at the other relationships in your life, you'll probably find a few more.

1. *Your Other Children:* "I think I could handle David's sleep problems," wrote Glen, "but I can't stand to watch what it's doing to his sister. Because of his crying, she's not getting the sleep she needs. And because my wife and I are both so tired, she's not getting the attention she deserves from us. I can't just let this go on, hoping that someday the baby will grow out of his awful sleep habits."

If you, like Glen, have a night crier *and* another child, your parenting problems are compounded. When there's another child who innocently bears the brunt of your fatigue, something inside you yells "Unfair!," and then the guilt begins to grow. It is unfair to deprive your other child of a patient and nurturing environment. It is also unfair when his normal sleep patterns are constantly disrupted by the night cries of a sibling.

When there are several children in the family, parents are often motivated to try sleep training in the name of fairness.

2. *Your Spouse:* It is very difficult to remain a loving and attentive spouse when nerve endings are raw and tempers are short. That's why, as we mentioned in chapter 1, many parents come to our Crying Baby Clinic for the sake of their marriage.

Sleepless nights provide fertile ground for the growth of misdirected anger. When couples don't understand why the baby is crying so much, they often blame each other. One parent wrote: "We're sure my neighbors know all about the baby's sleeping problem because we have had many loud fights over what is the best solution."

Another mother wrote: "I'm not sure why it happens, but when the baby cries my husband and I get mad at each other. Sometimes we find ourselves competing in terms of how much sleep we did or didn't get. I know this sounds silly, but I want him to know when I've suffered more than he has." Of course, blaming each other doesn't relieve the suffering, but it does give the anger a concrete target.

This anger often mixes with resentment to further damage the relationship. A mother wrote: "I'm very upset with my husband because he doesn't get up with the baby at all. I know he has to go to work in the morning, but so do I! Where is it written that the mother gets stuck with the nighttime duty?" Judging by the comments of couples who come to our clinic, we may conclude that this woman speaks for many mothers of night-crying babies.

Night-crying babies also can turn intimate, loving moments between a husband and wife into vague memories. Prolonged feelings of exhaustion and anger are sure to weaken anyone's sex drive. Sex can eventually become an impossible feat when, as one mother wrote, "The only thing I want to do in that bed is sleep! And, besides, my husband rarely even sleeps with me anymore. He says he gets a better night's sleep in the guest room. He can't hear the baby cry, and I don't disturb him when I'm getting up and down all night."

The anger and isolation these parents feel starts because of a crying baby, but it often grows into serious marital problems. It's a shame when this happens because there really is no reason for it. There *is* a solution to night crying.

3. *Your Unborn Children:* It's not farfetched to claim that a baby's night-crying habit may be responsible for making him the last child his parents will ever conceive. Obviously the lowered sex drive and infrequent opportunities that we just mentioned are partly to blame. But more damaging is the couple's fear that this could happen again. The very thought of two or three more years without sleep makes most parents at our clinic say, "Never again!"—and they mean it.

4. *Yourself:* Every parent of a night crier has at one time or another heard his or her little inner voice say, "What about me?" The relationship you have with yourself is very important. You need time to take care of and pamper yourself. You need to nurture your inner self so you'll have the stamina and fortitude to be a loving parent.

A night-crying baby, however, makes many parents lose sight of that inner being. He can make you doubt your competence as a parent. He can make you view yourself as a failure. And he can demand all of your time and energy. This can make you angry at the baby because, as one mother wrote: "I feel so irritated and annoyed. I feel like my daughter has totally consumed me. I start to cry every day when I look ahead to the night and the next day and realize there's going to be no relief for me."

The days and nights with a night crier do seem endless. Life becomes a series of small naps interrupted by cries that demand soothing. Many parents say they came to our clinic when that little inner voice grew into a loud, bellowing yell: "What about me!"

5. *Your Baby:* Sleep is a basic human need. As we mentioned earlier in this chapter, loss of sleep can cause you to feel angry.

If this anger and loss of sleep go on for a long time, however, the consequence may be a long-lasting negative effect on your relationship with your baby. The effect voiced by many parents is: "I'm so tired and irritable during the day that I lose my temper very quickly and yell at the baby for the slightest things. I don't even have the energy to play games or have fun with him anymore." This is not the kind of relationship these parents hoped to have with their babies, but that's what happens when they don't get enough sleep.

More serious problems can also develop when the chronic night crying breaks down the marital structure or damages your sense of self-esteem. One mother of a twenty-two-month-old son confessed her deepest secret through sobbing tears: "To be honest," she said, "sometimes I really hate this baby. If she cries through one more night, I'm scared by the thought of what I might do." Parents in a situation like this mother's are not surprised to learn that excessive crying is the trigger that sparks infant battering in 80 percent of the child abuse cases of children less than one year old. Anyone who laughs off your complaints with a flippant, "Babies are supposed to cry," has never lived with a night crier.

There is no doubt that parenting a night crier is difficult. But, as hard as this may be to believe, your baby is just as much a victim as you. He is doing something that causes you to withhold your love at the very moment he wants your complete love and attention. He really is innocent of any intentional malice; he loves you and needs your help to break his nighttime crying habit.

The next chapter will explain how you may have unknowingly taught him this bad habit, and it will show you how to use the Quick-Check Method to break it.

4

TEACHING YOUR BABY TO SLEEP THROUGH THE NIGHT

It's easy to believe we can teach our children to do things like talking, walking and clapping. It's also generally agreed we can teach our children that it's unacceptable to hit friends, kick the dog or break our good crystal. But teach our baby not to cry at night? Teach our baby how to fall asleep by himself? This may sound impossible, but it's not. Although crying is an inborn behavior, how often we cry, when we cry, and how long we cry can be *learned* behaviors. If you can accept this statement as a working hypothesis, then you can begin to change your baby's crying patterns.

The first step, then, to profiting from our program of sleep training is to treat your baby's night crying as a learned behavior. The second step is understanding how this behavior is learned. When you have an awareness of this learning process, you will better comprehend how activities like night crying can be *unlearned,* and how more appropriate behaviors can be learned in their place.

Your little night waker has already used the basic techniques of behavior modification to teach you how to soothe him to sleep. He has used his cries to train you how to respond to his nighttime needs. Maybe he wants another feeding, or maybe he likes to be rocked to sleep, or maybe he likes you to take him into your bed. He will keep crying until you respond with just the right sleep-inducing method. Even though your baby doesn't have the mental capacity to understand the principles of learning, he certainly does know that if he cries for your attention you'll come to him. In most circumstances this awareness is positive and necessary. But for the night waker it is most often negative and unnecessary.

You too unknowingly apply the principles of learning in your day-to-day activities. Without formal training or a doctor's degree, you teach your child to walk, talk, skip, hug, kiss and many other things. But by consistently attending to his night crying, you may have also taught him that he needs you to fall asleep. We know you haven't intentionally done anything to make your baby cry at night. You haven't been negligent—and you shouldn't feel guilty. But you do need to know some of the laws of learning so you can now change your baby's night-waking habit. Your baby needs you to take control, learn these principles, and teach him how to sleep by himself. This chapter will give you the skills to do just that.

Laws of Learning

1. *Consequences:* Most human behavior is learned. One of the methods by which we learn is based on the consequences that

follow our actions. Simply said this means: If you *reinforce* a behavior with a positive consequence, you can expect to see more of that behavior; if you *punish* a behavior with a negative consequence, you can expect to see less of that behavior.

Think about how this relates to your night-crying problem: You have *reinforced* your baby's nighttime dependence on you by responding to his call on demand, and he has learned to *punish* your absence from him by crying until he weakens your decision to ignore him. To break this power struggle, you now have to supply the third type of consequence to the baby's cry for control and *do nothing*. You want neither to reinforce the crying behavior nor to punish it. You want to end it.

The everyday methods we use to reinforce positive behaviors (like clapping hands, talking, waving bye-bye, and showing good manners) and to extinguish negative behaviors (like tantrums, hair pulling, swearing and hitting) are the very same techniques we apply to night crying. Pediatricians, for example, often suggest that parents ignore negative behaviors like head banging and temper tantrums. They even caution parents that the undesirable behavior may get worse at first but promise that when the child learns that these actions no longer get attention, he will stop.

Teaching your baby to sleep with our method is just an extension of this kind of discipline. If you feel comfortable and confident ignoring a temper tantrum despite the initial screaming you have to endure, then you are already involved in the technique used for sleep training.

When you first use the Quick-Check Method of sleep training, your baby's night crying will probably escalate into screams. He will try anything to get you into his room to comfort him as you have done every night in the past. Screaming, head banging, breath holding, vomiting, toy throwing, etc., will all be attempts to make you come into his room. The Quick-Check Method will show you how not to respond to these nighttime tantrums with comfort and attention.

2. *Association:* Another way that we learn is through association. That is, if two things happen at the same time or close together (i.e., are associated), then we tend to expect them to occur together again.

We have all learned to associate many things with sleeping. It is not a biological fact that some of us cannot sleep unless the room is dark, or the sheets are pulled up to our chins, or the pillow is folded in half. But if we have associated the state of sleep with one or many of these things, our sleep will be disturbed if one or more of these conditions is suddenly missing. Children too learn to associate various conditions or things with falling asleep. They may mentally connect their bedroom, crib or bed, a special blanket or a doll with the act of falling asleep. Once the association has been made, they need these conditions present when they fall asleep. They also need them present in order to go back to sleep when they wake in the middle of the night. So when the child has made sleep associations that rely on a condition not present when he awakens in the middle of the night, he cannot get back to sleep without it. He then becomes a night crier.

For example:

· Nine-month-old Kara associates sleep with her mother's warm body and rhythmic rocking because her mother enjoys rocking her to sleep every night. But when Kara wakes later in the night, she cannot get back to sleep because her mother is no longer rocking or holding her. Kara is a night crier who needs her mother to help her fall asleep.

· Seven-month-old Judy has learned to associate sucking on a pacifier with falling asleep. This is why she screams for her parents each time she wakes. She needs them to put the pacifier back into her mouth.

· Six-month-old Danny associates sleep with nursing at his mother's breast. Although he no longer needs to nurse every few hours throughout the night for nourishment, it is the only way he can fall back to sleep.

· Bottle-fed David has the same problem. At eighteen months he also no longer needs a night feeding, but he wants a bottle when he goes to bed. Because his parents worry that leaving the bottle in David's mouth while he sleeps will cause tooth decay, they remove it from the crib after he falls asleep. What else can David do but cry when he wakes up and finds no bottle there to help him fall back to sleep?

· Twenty-two-month-old Lauren likes to have one of her parents sit at the bottom of her bed until she falls asleep. Sometimes this takes more than an hour, but she screams if no one is there. Lauren is also a night crier because when she wakes during the night, the prop that she associates with sleep is no longer there.

If your baby has developed an incorrect sleep association like these children and you have continually offered the consequence of returning the missing sleep prop each time he cries, it should now be clear to you that his night crying is a learned behavior and that you are a part of the problem.

Once you understand that you have taught your baby poor sleep associations and you know how this learning occurred, you should have the confidence to teach him successfully the new sleep associations that will help him sleep without calling out for you. (For more information on behavior management, see the list of suggested readings in the bibliography.)

Now that you understand better the techniques of behavior modification we will use in this sleep training program, it's time to ask yourself again: Do I honestly want my baby to learn how to fall asleep without my help? We hope this background knowledge of how people learn has helped you set aside any doubts you may have had and has helped you to answer the question with a confident and resounding "Yes!"

The Quick-Check Method

Sleep training is a controversial issue. Our program grew out of a personal need when one of our own children became a chronic night waker thirteen years ago. At that time there were only two schools of thought on how to handle this problem. The "hard liners" believed that you should let the child cry it out for however long it takes before the child stops and falls asleep. The trouble with this approach is that the child may cry harder and longer if he thinks he's been deserted by his parents. It is also so hard on the parents and the baby that most families give up after the first few hours. On the other hand, the "softies" believed that you should immediately comfort a crying baby, no matter when the baby cries. The difficulty here is that one can indeed spoil children over six months old by giving them attention they do not need. You too have probably heard of these techniques and are confused by such opposite views. Our program takes the middle ground between these two extreme remedies and is supported by the most recent sleep disorder research. This kind of approach is also supported by sleep specialists Richard Ferber, M.D., and Christopher Green, M.D.

If your baby is a night waker, it's important to remember that we all wake several times in the course of a night. Your goal is not to make your baby sleep longer but to develop sleep patterns that won't disturb *you* in the middle of the night.

We believe that after six months babies can learn behaviors like crying and sleeping. You may already have taught your baby how to cry at night. This Quick-Check Method can now help you teach him how to sleep.

Procedure

1. Pick a bedtime when your child typically shows signs of sleepiness. Once you have decided on a reasonable time, don't vary it from night to night. A consistent bedtime will help establish a regular sleep-wake rhythm in your child. So if 8:00 PM is bedtime, be sure your child is in bed at 8:00 and not 8:20, 8:10 or 7:45.

2. Establish a quiet, relaxing bedtime ritual, such as giving a bath, putting on a sleeper, playing music, reading a book or singing a lullaby. Then say goodnight and leave. This should be a comforting time alone with one parent to help the child unwind and prepare for sleep. Begin the routine at a set bedtime, follow the same sequence of events, and allow it to take about twenty minutes each night.

3. Once you have finished your bedtime ritual, say good night and leave the bedroom *before your child is asleep*. Keep reminding yourself that your baby is capable of falling asleep on his own without your help. You just have to teach him how. So don't rock or pat him to sleep and don't give him a feeding.

The child's bedroom should be exactly the same in the middle of the night as when he falls asleep. There should be no parent around, no overhead light on, no music playing, and so on. If the bedroom environment remains the same when the child awakens at night, he will learn to associate it with sleep.

4. If your child cries when you leave at bedtime or awakens crying at night, wait five minutes before responding. Then go and make a quick check on him to reassure yourself that he is all right. This quick check should be just that—*quick*. Stay with the baby only one or two minutes to clean up any mess or to make sure he is not feverish, in pain, too hot or too cold. Do not pick him up, argue or attempt to persuade. Rather:

a. go up close to him;

b. establish eye contact;

c. maintain a stern facial expression;

d. use a firm voice to say his name and give a simple, direct command such as, "Go to sleep";

e. do not scream, become hostile, or hit him;

f. do not sympathize, hug or show your distress.

If the crying persists for another twenty minutes after the first check, go again to check on your child and remind him that you expect sleep, not crying, at this hour. Do not feed, rock or pick him up when you check. Leave again before he is asleep.

Repeat this procedure of briefly checking on your child after every twenty-minute crying spell for as long as it takes him to finally get tired and fall asleep. If your child is crying softly or whimpering at the end of a twenty-minute period, do not go and check because he is probably close to falling asleep on his own.

By checking on the child every twenty minutes, you are not only reassuring yourself that nothing is physically wrong with him, but you are also letting the child know that he has not been abandoned. This will alleviate any extreme nighttime anxiety that would keep a child wakeful and fearful.

Twenty minutes seems to be the optimal length of time to let infant night wakers cry. On many occasions they will fall back to sleep on their own after ten to fifteen minutes of crying. Such brief crying episodes seem to release tension and allow the child to fall back to sleep. Longer intervals (eg., forty-five to sixty minutes) seem like an eternity to both parents and baby.

5. Awaken your baby at his usual wake time in the morning. Do not allow him to sleep any later regardless of how little sleep you or he had the night before. Also, keep his daily nap schedule intact. Do not allow him to take more or longer naps during the day. This would only disturb the wake/sleep rhythms you're trying to develop to ensure a good night's sleep.

6. You can expect the first night's crying to be the worst. Typically a child will cry loudly for one or two hours. Some will cry less and a few will cry off and on for almost the entire night.

The second night should bring a slight reduction in the total crying time. The third night should result in a significant reduction in the crying, as the child learns to soothe himself and put himself back to sleep. We have found that after three nights of this procedure, most children learn to sleep through without any "checking" required by the parents. Some will continue to wake once or twice, cry briefly, and then go back to sleep on their own. A few children show some progress after three nights but need a week or two of the program before they learn to sleep through. These are children who do not adapt readily to any new procedure.

7. Rather than actively listening to your baby cry at night, use earplugs to muffle the sound. Some parents close several doors as a noise abatement procedure; others go outside to escape the noise. (See chapter 6 for more noise abatement techniques.)

8. Make a commitment to follow this program for a minimum of three nights. Then be absolutely consistent in adhering to the procedures. Don't give in—no matter how much your baby cries. If your baby vomits after agitated crying, go in quickly to clean up the mess and then leave before he is asleep.

9. Begin the program when it is most convenient for you. Many parents have found Friday night to be a good time to start because they do not have to worry about going to work on the weekends. Others have found it best to start the program during naptime. They have found it easier to tolerate crying during the day, and it's easier on spouses and neighbors.

10. At naptime follow the same procedure of leaving before your child is asleep. If your child cries, go in and make a quick check after five minutes. Then check again every twenty minutes thereafter if vigorous crying continues. If your child is still crying after an hour, remove him from the crib and say that naptime is over. Do not let the child fall asleep at any time other than naptime or at any place other than the crib. If your child falls asleep despite your best efforts to keep him awake, allow him to sleep only ten to fifteen minutes and then awaken him.

Establish a regular schedule for naptimes. Children less than a year old tend to nap twice a day. Children older than one year generally take one midday nap around noontime. Do not let your child nap late in the day, say 4:00 PM or later.

11. Keep a record of the length of time your child cries, using the blank charts in Appendix A. There are several reasons for writing down the crying time. Because you are emotionally involved in the sleep-training process, it is almost impossible to remember accurately the duration of each crying episode. When every minute seems like an hour, it's also difficult to be sure that twenty minutes have in fact passed since the last quick check. Writing down the total crying time for each night will also help you see concrete progress each day. Thirty minutes of crying on the second night *feels* just as awful as fifty minutes of crying on the first night, but your written record will objectively reassure you of progress.

Bryan Johnson, at 10 months, didn't wake up after he went to sleep, but he would go to sleep only if one of his parents was standing over his crib, patting his back, and singing a lullaby. His parents, Sandy and John, wanted to end this ritual which often took more than an hour. The chart on pages 57–59 shows a record of their progress with the Quick-Check Method.

On the first night, Bryan was put to bed at 8:00 PM. When his parents said good night and left without any patting or singing, Bryan jumped to his feet crying.

At 8:05, Sandy went into Bryan's room for the first quick check. She stayed only a minute, checking to be sure he was physically safe and comfortable. Then she left. Sandy recorded the five minutes of crying between the 8:00 bedtime and the 8:05 quick check.

At 8:25 it was John's turn to make a quick check on Bryan, who was still crying. When he left Bryan's room, he recorded the twenty minutes of crying between the 8:05 check and the 8:25 check. This continued until Bryan finally fell asleep at 9:15. They recorded a total crying time of seventy-five minutes for the first night.

On the second night Sandy and John were discouraged because Bryan cried even longer than on the first, but he finally did go to sleep after an hour and a half of crying and quick checks. When Sandy called us the next morning to report this "failure," we assured her that a regression like this is very common. We encouraged her to continue using the Quick-Check Method.

Each night after that, Sandy and John again kept a careful record of crying and checking. Although Bryan continued to cry in protest, on the third night (as their chart shows) they saw a decrease in his crying time. Then on the fourth night Bryan went into his bed at 8:00 PM and went right to sleep.

Eighteen-month-old Jason, on the other hand, always went to bed around 9:30 PM with no problem. But he would then wake continually throughout the rest of the night. Jason's mum had

Bryan Quick-Check Chart

	Night #1	Night #2	Night #3	Night #4	Night #5	Night #6	Night #7
	Quick-Check Time	Quick-Check Time	Quick-Check Time	Quick-Check Time	Quick-Check Time	Quick-Check Time	Quick-Check Time
Start of Crying Time	8:00 PM	8:00 PM	8:00 PM				
Check #1	8:05	8:05	8:05				
Check #2	8:25	8:25					
Check #3	8:45	8:45					
Check #4	9:05	9:05					
Check #5		9:25					
Check #6							
Check #7							
Sleeptime	9:15	9:30	8:20				
Total Crying Time	75 minutes	90 minutes	20 minutes				

	Night #1	Night #2	Night #3	Night #4	Night #5	Night #6	Night #7
	Quick-Check Time	Quick-Check Time	Quick-Check Time	Quick-Check Time	Quick-Check Time	Quick-Check Time	Quick-Check Time
Wake-up #1							
Check #1							
Check #2							
Check #3							
Check #4							
Check #5							
Check #6							
Check #7							
Sleeptime							
Total Crying Time							

	Night #1	Night #2	Night #3	Night #4	Night #5	Night #6	Night #7
	Quick-Check Time	Quick-Check Time	Quick-Check Time	Quick-Check Time	Quick-Check Time	Quick-Check Time	Quick-Check Time
Wake-up #2							
Check #1							
Check #2							
Check #3							
Check #4							
Check #5							
Check #6							
Check #7							
Sleeptime							
Total Crying Time							

nursed him and found it easiest to handle the night feedings by taking him into her bed. But when Jason no longer needed night feedings, he still wanted to sleep in his parents' bed. Now Claire and her husband, George, wanted him to sleep through the night in his crib.

On the first night, Jason went into his crib as usual at 9:40 PM without any problems. When he awoke at 10:30 PM expecting to go into his parent's bed, Claire and George began teaching him how to sleep by himself. They checked on him five minutes after the crying began and then recorded the time of the crying and the time of the first check. The chart on pages 61–63 shows a record of their sleep training period.

Jason continued to cry. Twenty minutes later Claire and George made another quick check and then left his room. They again recorded the time of the check and the length of the crying time. They continued to do this until Jason fell asleep at 11:25 PM. They recorded a total of fifty-five minutes of crying and checking.

Jason awoke for the second time at 1:15 AM. Again he cried to go into his parents' bed. Claire and George recorded the time of each quick check until Jason fell asleep at 1:45 AM after a total crying time of thirty minutes. Claire and George repeated this process when Jason again woke at 3:15 AM and cried until 3:20. When Jason woke again at 6:30 AM, Claire decided that was enough for one night and took Jason to the playroom to start his day.

On the second and third nights, Claire and George again kept a careful record of Jason's progress. Despite their tired outlook, they had a physical record that showed Jason was indeed learning to sleep for longer periods by himself. By the fourth night Jason slept straight through without calling for his parents.

Jason Quick-Check Chart

	Night #1	Night #2	Night #3	Night #4	Night #5	Night #6	Night #7
	Quick-Check Time	Quick-Check Time	Quick-Check Time	Quick-Check Time	Quick-Check Time	Quick-Check Time	Quick-Check Time
Start of Crying Time	10:30 PM	12:00 AM	4:20 AM				
Check #1	10:35	12:05					
Check #2	10:55	12:25					
Check #3	11:15						
Check #4							
Check #5							
Check #6							
Check #7							
Sleeptime	11:25	12:35	4:25				
Total Crying Time	55 minutes	35 minutes	5 minutes				

	Night #1	Night #2	Night #3	Night #4	Night #5	Night #6	Night #7
	Quick-Check Time	Quick-Check Time	Quick-Check Time	Quick-Check Time	Quick-Check Time	Quick-Check Time	Quick-Check Time
Wake-up #1							
Check #1	1:15 AM	4:20 AM	7:00 AM				
Check #2	1:20	4:25					
Check #3	1:40						
Check #4							
Check #5							
Check #6							
Check #7							
Sleeptime	1:45	4:30					
Total Crying Time	30 minutes	10 minutes					

	Night #1	Night #2	Night #3	Night #4	Night #5	Night #6	Night #7
	Quick-Check Time	Quick-Check Time	Quick-Check Time	Quick-Check Time	Quick-Check Time	Quick-Check Time	Quick-Check Time
Wake-up #2	3:15 AM	7:00 AM					
Check #1							
Check #2							
Check #3							
Check #4							
Check #5							
Check #6							
Check #7							
Sleeptime	3:20						
Total Crying Time	5 minutes						
Wake-up #3	6:30 AM						

Use the blank charts in appendix A to keep track of your baby's sleep patterns on each night of the program. You may not feel very successful when you're filling in the blanks at 2:00 AM, but your chart will be proof that things are getting better.

Complications

If Your Baby Sleeps in a Bed

A lot of parents have come to us with the same concern. "How can I use the Quick-Check Method," they ask, "if my child sleeps in a bed and runs out of the room?"

Mary, for example, realized she was reinforcing an unnecessary sleep association by lying down next to twenty-six-month-old Beth in order to get her to sleep each night. She was sure that the Quick-Check Method was just what she needed to end this time-consuming ritual. But then Mary gave in to Beth's crying after just fifteen minutes. "It may be one thing to leave a baby crying in the secure confines of a crib, but Beth kept running out of the room until I finally locked her in. I could hear her running around the darkened room, frantically looking for some way out. I just couldn't stand it."

It is indeed more difficult to use the Quick-Check Method with a night crier who can run out the door faster than you can turn out the light, but there are a number of ways to handle this problem with a management technique called limit setting. Limit setting can be taught at the same time you're teaching your child to sleep.

One way to set limits for your child is to consistently and

persistently return him to his bed. This is a tiring process because it can go on all night long for three or four nights, but eventually it will work. The method is simple: escort your child back to his bed *every time* he comes out; do this quickly (no more than ten seconds) with little discussion (no more than ten words). Remember:

· Don't sympathize with his problem.
· Don't scold him for being bad.
· Don't argue.
· Don't linger in his room.
· Don't beg for his cooperation.
· Don't permit glasses of water.
· Don't give last-minute hugs.
· Don't read "one more" story.
· Be firm.
· Be confident.
· Be determined.
· Be consistent.

When your child realizes that you aren't going to change your mind and that you are not going to reward his behavior with anything positive, the behavior will stop.

Another way to handle a child who sprints from the room is to chain-lock the door. You may feel, like Mary, that this is too cruel. But when it is done with the proper precautions and intent, it is an effective and perfectly acceptable way to teach children who are eighteen months and older.

Before bedtime, make your child's room completely child-proof. Because he may get angry enough to throw things or hurt himself, be sure to remove all breakable and sharp objects.

Also check to see if the dresser, shelf or toy box needs to be bolted to the wall so he can't pull it down on himself. Install smoke alarms as well.

Now put a chain lock on the outside of the door. A chain lock will allow your child to open the door, call out and maintain contact with the outside world, but it sets a limit to his wanderings.

On the first night of sleep training, tell your child that if he comes out of his room, you will have to use the lock. If he comes out anyway, return him to his room, leave on a night light, and use the chain lock. Tell him that when he gets into his bed, you'll take the chain off. When he returns to his bed, take it off. If he comes back out of the room, put it back on. Do not put the lock on for the night and walk away. You must take it off each time your child gets into his bed so he'll realize he has control over the situation. This feeling of control makes the locked door less scary and puts the final verdict of an open or closed door in his hands: if he stays in bed, the door is open; if he gets out of bed, the door is locked.

You cannot make your child go to sleep, but you can set the limit that he must stay in his bed. Maintain your schedule of quick checks to assure his safety and ease his fear of abandonment. If he should fall asleep on the floor while crying, don't worry about it. At least he has fallen asleep in his own room without the props he was accustomed to.

A variation of this limit-setting technique is to *hold* the door shut from the other side. Explain to your child that you will let go and open the door when he gets back into bed. Obviously this requires more personal involvement on your part, but it still lets your child know he has control over the door.

You might also want to try limit setting by placing a gate in the doorway. Most children, however, find a way to climb over one or to knock it down.

When teaching the Quick-Check Method to these children, the original rules about attitude still apply. Many parents find it difficult to keep their tempers with a child who won't stay in bed. It's still important, however, to remain calm, firm and confident. Don't scream at or hit your child—he needs your help and support. If your child is at least two and a half years old, you might even encourage him to stay in bed by offering him some kind of concrete reward.

Jim and Sally found that a star chart helped their three-year-old Eric learn to stay in his bed and sleep through the night. Eric and his mother made a calendar to record his progress. Each time he stayed in bed all night, he received a gold star. When he earned three gold stars, he was given a special treat at the ice-cream parlor.

You can use any reward you feel would motivate your child, but there are a few rules to keep in mind:

· Make sure your child understands *exactly* what he must do to earn the reward.
· Once you've agreed on the necessary behavior, don't bargain. Don't change the ground rules and decide to give a reward for "trying."
· Don't ever take away a reward that's been earned.
· If your child doesn't earn the reward, don't scold him. Let the attainment of the reward be his responsibility and totally in his control; you can be supportive and sympathetic.

Is this bribery? We don't think so. Giving a reward for accomplishing a difficult task helps a child get over the initial hurdle. Then when the behavior is well established, the reward system should be slowly phased out.

Night Weaning

Another complication some parents must deal with while using the Quick-Check Method is weaning their child from night feedings. There is usually no nutritional need for night feedings after three or four months. So if your night crier is still feeding on demand throughout the night, it is probably because he has learned to associate going to sleep with bottle or breast sucking. This is further complicated by a physical problem: when the habit of night feedings is established, the baby will wake with hunger pains even though he does not need food. This happens because his internal clock has *learned* this schedule.

If your sleep is constantly disturbed because your baby "needs" to be fed, you actually have two problems to overcome. You have to train your baby to eat on a daytime schedule, and then you must break the association he has made between sleep and food. Use the following suggestions—together with the information in chapter 2—to help you do just that:

· After six months of age don't nurse or bottle-feed your baby to sleep. An early-evening feeding is all right, but just make sure the baby is awake when you put him to bed. Many mothers enjoy rocking and feeding their babies to sleep. But when the baby learns to demand these conditions to fall back to sleep in the middle of the night, the habit becomes disruptive.

· Never put a baby to bed with a bottle. This may cause a middle ear problem and may contribute to tooth decay. It is also the cause of night crying for babies who wake and can't find their bottle. They call out for you to reestablish the conditions they associate with falling asleep.
· If your baby is taking four or more ounces at his night feedings, it is best to wean your baby gradually from this habit. You should start by reducing the baby's intake by a half ounce at each feeding on the first night. Nursing mothers should cut feeding time back by half a minute each night and should also increase the time between feedings by a half hour each night.

Some parents find they can cut back on their baby's demand for a bottle by gradually diluting its contents. Eventually the baby is given only water in the bottle. At that point many babies lose interest in it. Even if your baby doesn't, you can stop the night feedings confident that he is not crying from hunger.

Many parents ask, "Will it help my baby sleep through the night if I give more solid foods, like cereal, during the day or before he goes to bed at night?" The answer is *probably not*. But if your pediatrician agrees, you might want to give it a try. However, because the baby's night wakings are generally caused by hunger pains that have nothing to do with nutritional needs, a bit of cereal won't stop the night crying.

Pitfalls

Sometimes parents leave our Crying Baby Clinic determined to do whatever is necessary to teach their baby how to sleep.

Then they come back a few weeks later feeling angry and betrayed. They claim to have used our Quick-Check Method, and yet their baby is still crying through the night.

After talking with many of these parents, we have found several common pitfalls that can sabotage our method. To avoid these same disappointments, read through each of the following problems faced by other parents before beginning the Quick-Check Method.

Lack of Consistency

Attitude: Julie and her husband, Dan, were sure they had followed our program to the letter. They checked on one-year-old Billy only when they were supposed to. Each check lasted no more than a minute. They didn't pick him up, offer him a bottle or pat his back to soothe him. When we probed further, however, we found that their attitude was reinforcing his crying. During each check they were overly sympathetic and showed undue concern. Although they never picked up Billy, they would often hug him and assure him that they knew how awful he must feel. This was enough feedback for Billy to persist in his attempt for continued attention.

Your attitude must be consistently firm and confident. This will take a conscious effort on your part because sometimes your heart will be breaking with concern, and other times you'll feel angry and resentful.

Consistently follow the procedure outlined in no. 4 of the Quick-Check Method. And don't underestimate your infant's ability to understand your directions. Our experience supports the research findings of Doctors Michael Meyerhoff and Burton L. White, which state that the capacity of normal children to understand simple words and instructions begins well before the first birthday, usually when they are between six and nine months old. Unfortunately many parents don't give directions or commands to children who can't talk back and acknowledge the instructions.

Babies of all ages can also detect any trace of doubt or ambivalence in your approach. Once they sense you're not sure about teaching this lesson, you've weakened the chances of a behavior change.

A firm and confident attitude is an important factor in assuring the success of this program.

Sometimes yes, Sometimes no: Once you begin to teach your baby how to sleep without your help, the lesson must be consistently reinforced at *every* sleep time. Consider eleven-month-old Dorrie. Her parents could no longer stand having to rock her to sleep in the living room every night, so they decided to try the Quick-Check Method. On the first night, Dorrie cried for almost two hours. On the second night the crying time was reduced to thirty-five minutes. On the third night Dorrie's grandmother stopped in for an unexpected visit. Rather than ruin the night with more crying, Dorrie's parents decided to skip the sleep training just for this one night, and Dorrie again fell asleep on her mother's lap in the living room.

Unfortunately Dorrie had no way of knowing that her parents hadn't really given up on what seemed to be some crazy plan to let her cry. In her mind the training had failed and the rocking routine was back. Both Dorrie and her parents were surprised when on the fourth night she again had to cry for two hours before falling asleep.

Parents who skip a night here and there because, for example, they're tired, or feeling sick, or having company, are inviting failure. Just as you cannot expect extinction of temper tantrums if you only ignore them occasionally, so it is with night crying. The behavior must be consistently ignored by everyone involved in the baby's sleep schedule.

I'm not going to do it—you do it: Both Marie and her husband, Joe, acknowledged the need to sleep train their ten-month-old daughter. Marie took on the task of putting Lisa to bed and going to her room for the quick checks. Although Joe supported the idea, he didn't want to be the one to walk away from the crying baby. This arrangement worked well until Marie had to be away from the house on the fourth night of the training period. Just when Lisa was learning to accept independent sleep habits, the bedtime routine changed. Her daddy presented a whole new chance to be rocked to sleep once again. Despite Joe's honest attempt to keep the routine going, his late arrival in the process—combined with his anxious attitude—caused a setback in Lisa's progress. Her crying time returned to the time recorded on the first night.

If both parents are available at the baby's bedtime, the ideal solution is for both parents to support the program actively by taking turns checking. If there is a grandparent, babysitter or other person who is occasionally involved in the baby's sleep schedule, try to involve him or her in the training process also. If the baby knows that the rules apply no matter who puts him to sleep, you can avoid this kind of regression.

Too Sick to Cry?

Sometimes after a long period of crying, a child may become hysterical and vomit. At this point, Lorraine and Pete gave in.

They removed sixteen-month-old Sharon from her crib to stop her crying because, as they said, "We can't let a sick baby cry."

If this happens with your baby, it's important to remember that you do not have a sick child on your hands. This hysterical vomiting is the baby's way of increasing negative behavior to make you give in. This is not a medical problem; the baby is making himself sick. One of the reasons for checking every twenty minutes is to take care of this kind of episode. There is never a reason for the baby to be physically uncomfortable.

To hold the line during this escalation period, however, you must maintain your firm attitude. Matter-of-factly clean up the mess as quickly as possible, and then leave the room. It is usually not necessary to change the baby's clothes and linens completely. If you spend too much time attending to the mess, then the baby has won the reward of attention.

Midnight Acrobatics

Eight-month-old Carrie cried thirty minutes less on the second night than she did on the first night of sleep training. Her mother, Sue, was pleased with the progress and was sure Carrie would eventually sleep through the night. Then on the third night, Sue found Carrie standing in the crib for the first time, with no idea how to get down. "Every time I went in to check, she'd be standing there looking so helpless and stranded," said Sue the next morning. "I couldn't leave knowing she'd climb right back up and be stuck there for twenty more minutes. So I gave up and took her into my bed."

Was this sabotage or a real developmental problem? Whatever the case, we advised Sue to spend time during the day teaching Carrie how to get down from the standing position by bending her knees and helping her to sit. With practice, a child can learn this skill in just a few days; then it's time to get back to the business of sleep training.

Other parents have found it difficult to continue sleep training when they found their children with their feet and legs stuck through the crib bars. This is why you need to check every twenty minutes—to assure physical comfort. This problem gives you a reason to be glad you're checking but not a reason to give up.

Many parents also worry that their baby will put himself in danger by trying to climb out of the crib. If that's your concern, don't give up trying to teach good sleep habits—just assure the baby's safety by putting a mattress or some pillows on the floor around the crib and continue with the program. If the baby does learn to climb out of the crib and comes running after you, as children in beds often do, then it's time to use the limit-setting technique explained earlier in this chapter.

Unrealistic Expectations

It is unrealistic to expect instant and unwavering success. Learning any new skill takes time, practice and reinforcement. Independent sleep habits are no exception. The actual time it will take your baby to learn to put himself to sleep is an individual matter. Some babies will learn in two or three nights; others will take a full week. As a general rule, you should see a reduction in the crying time after three nights and a steady reduction each night thereafter. Most babies will be self-soothing within one week. If there is absolutely no change in the crying time after one full week of using our method, then we recommend stopping the procedure to reevaluate any possible pitfalls or medical problems. If there is no apparent reason for the continued crying, then your baby may be one of the exceptions to the rule that we will discuss in chapter 5.

It is also unrealistic not to expect occasional relapses. No learned behavior is ironclad, especially with the one- to three-year-old. Consider tantrums, toilet training or room cleaning. Even after we have successfully taught our child what is expected and acceptable, there are usually times of regression. A sudden change, such as in the baby's health, environment or schedule, may also bring on a relapse of night crying. These relapses will be short-lived, however, if you handle them in the same firm, consistent manner of the original training period.

Lack of Commitment

A lack of total commitment to the program is the most difficult problem for parents to overcome. They want their baby to be an independent sleeper, but there are other factors that can sabotage their efforts.

Joan, for example, found it impossible to continue using our method. Her husband did not believe it could work and really didn't mind the fact that nine-month-old Peter slept in their bed. This lack of spousal support quickly undermined Joan's commitment and she brought Peter back to their bed after only an hour and a half of crying and quick checks.

Jim, on the other hand, was very anxious for his eighteen-month-old daughter to sleep through the night because chronic lack of sleep was affecting his work. When he mentioned his enthusiasm for the Quick-Check Method to his mother, however, she was shocked that he planned to let his baby cry. "Babies only cry," she said, "because it's God's way of telling you they need you." This was enough to change Jim's mind.

Even the slightest hint of disapproval from a relative, friend or neighbor can cause parents who are not totally committed to falter in their intention to see the program through for the sake of the baby.

Most damaging to a parent's commitment is the baby's cry itself. No matter how well intentioned you may be, if you can't stand to hear your baby cry, this approach is going to be tough on your sense of commitment.

A belief in the basic philosophy of sleep training is very important. When we meet with parents who don't really believe that their baby can be taught how to sleep, we expect the baby to come out the winner. Babies seem able to cry longer than uncertain parents can hold out.

These pitfalls are the ones we find most often interfere with our sleep-training method. Because you and your baby are unique individuals, you may run into problems we haven't included here. But whatever the difficulties, keep reminding yourself that it takes time and patience to teach your baby any new skill. Independent sleep is a skill that can be taught by a loving teacher who is firm, consistent, realistic and committed.

5

EXCEPTIONS TO THE RULE

The Quick-Check Method of sleep training has been developed to help children who have poor sleeping habits. It teaches parents how to break their baby's habit of depending on some external prop to induce sleep, and it teaches the baby how to replace that dependency with the natural ability to put himself to sleep. We want to help you and your baby sleep through the night, but you must first determine *why* your baby isn't sleeping as you feel he should. If your child is a night waker because the two of you have developed some bad sleeping habits, then the Quick-Check Method is your ticket to a good night's sleep. But there are also cases of disturbed sleep patterns in children for which the Quick-Check Method is not an appropriate solution. This chapter will describe ten such sleep problems which cannot be resolved with the Quick-Check Method. We have also offered advice on how to handle each of these problems.

Nightmares

A nightmare is an anxiety-producing dream. If your child occasionally awakens in the middle of the night crying out in fear, this, of course, would not be an appropriate time to ignore his cries until he falls back to sleep on his own.

Nightmares usually begin to occur sometime between eighteen months and three years of age. At this time the child will cry out, but he is easily comforted and quickly quiets down. Nightmares often increase in frequency and severity in children four to five years old. These dreams are typically filled with feelings of helplessness and danger, and they are commonly about running away from wild animals or monsters. It's interesting to note that after age ten incidents of nightmares drop off rapidly.

What You Should Do: To calm the upset caused by occasional nightmares, give your child comfort and support with the following:

- Help your child awaken fully.
- Turn on a light to show him familiar surroundings.
- Hold and cuddle him.
- Remain calm and confident while talking soothingly and reassuringly.
- Talk about the dream.
- Explain that dreams are not real; they are make-believe.
- Let him know that everyone has scary dreams and that they can't hurt us.
- Reassure him that you're nearby and that you won't let anything happen to him.
- The next day you might try to teach him how to cope with nightmares by suggesting that if the bad dream returns, he can call on his favorite superhero for help, or he can make friends with the scary monster or animal.

· Avoid frightening movies at bedtime.
· Make a time for cuddling and closeness in your bedtime ritual.
· Do not start bad sleep habits by sharing your bed with your child when he is frightened. If he needs your closeness to fall back to sleep, stay in his room with him.

It is not common for children to suffer the distress of nightmares night after night. If your child has a recurring problem, it could be a sign that he is feeling a lot of stress, and you may need to consider professional counseling.

Night Terrors

Some children suffer a severe panic reaction (night terrors) when they arouse from a deep sleep state to a lighter one. Night terrors are characterized by frantic thrashing about in bed; wide-open, glassy, and unfocused eyes; elevated heart and respiration rates; and sometimes a panicky scream, accompanying a hallucination of some frightening image, such as a bug on the wall. All the while, they are in the state of sleep.

Instances of night terrors usually peak at ages three and four, but we have found that they can begin as early as six to eight months. It is believed that these terrors are not a sign of emotional disturbance but, rather, that they are physiological in origin—probably due to an immature sleep/wake mechanism. Children who experience these terrors usually have a family history of similar occurrences. Night terrors often come in spurts; a child may experience them once a month for three months and then not at all for six months.

What You Should Do: Night terrors are different from nightmares in that the child is not awake while experiencing a night terror and should not be held or comforted. If you try to hold him, he will probably try to push you away. It is best just to sit close by and observe and not awaken the child. Most cases of night terrors last from five to ten minutes, although some may go on for as long as thirty minutes or more. When these pass, the child will fall back into a peaceful sleep. Because some children may fall out of bed, hit their heads against the wall, or even run around the room, it is important to be nearby to assure their safety. Fortunately most children do not remember these episodes. So unless the child asks about it, don't talk about the night terror the next day.

Since night terrors are more likely to occur when a child is very tired, under stress or suffering from a fever, you can try to avoid their recurrence in an overly tired child by scheduling a nap or resttime each day and by reducing any environmental factors which may be causing stress.

Sleepwalking

Sleepwalking is a sleep disturbance very similar to night terrors. The sleepwalking child is not fully awake, but his eyes are open, glassy and unfocused. The occurrence will last just a few minutes, although some can go on for more than thirty minutes. The sleeper will not remember the incident in the morning, and it is best not to awaken him.

Studies have found that an estimated 15 percent of all children will sleepwalk at least once, and sleepwalking that starts before the age of ten is usually outgrown by the age of fifteen. It is also found that sleepwalking typically occurs during the first three hours of sleep and only once a night. Children who are extremely tired and have a high fever are more likely to walk in their sleep.

What You Should Do: The best approach is simply to lead the child gently back to bed without waking him. If he resists your efforts and wakes up, he will be confused and disoriented. You can then help him wake more fully by saying his name over and over, but don't slap him or throw cold water on him.

Your main job is to protect a sleepwalker from harm. Put a gate across the doorway. Put away any dangerous objects that may be in his room, and keep the windows shut.

Because tiredness seems to increase the likelihood of sleep-walking, try to have your child nap or rest every day if he is prone to such incidents.

Separation Anxiety

Preschool children (ages one to four) may cry at night because of intense separation anxiety. It will take some detective work on your part to decide if your child wants you nearby at night because it's a habit that the two of you have developed or a real fear of separation. If your child also reacts to daytime separation with severe panic and fear, then you will probably need to begin a program of desensitization to end his nighttime crying.

What You Should Do:

1. For the first three nights, sit near (not on) your baby's bed until he falls asleep. Let him know you don't expect to do this

for a long time because you know that eventually he won't need you to help him fall asleep.

2. Move your chair to the doorway for the following three nights and repeat the same positive message that soon he won't need you to help him fall asleep.

3. Continue moving further and further away in three-night intervals—outside the door, down the hall, down the stairs. When your child cries out for you, don't go to his bedside. Just call back "Go to sleep," in a firm, confident voice. Do not yell in anger or show undue concern. The child must know that if he doesn't stay in bed and go to sleep, then you won't sit there. If he won't stay in bed or in the room, then it's time for limit setting, which was explained in chapter 4.

Scheduling

Just like adults, children can't sleep unless they're tired. We have found that some babies can't sleep at night simply because they're on a poor wake/sleep schedule. You will be most successful in training your baby to sleep if you work with his natural sleep patterns.

Judy is a teacher. Her babysitter always put seven-month-old Sean down for his morning nap at 10:00 AM. Judy would then put him down for his afternoon nap when she came home from school at 3:00 PM. This schedule worked very well until Sean turned eighteen months old. Judy suddenly had a terrible time getting him to sleep at his usual 8:00 PM bedtime. She spent every night for one month fighting with a screaming baby. When she brought Sean to our clinic, we did not recommend the Quick-Check Method but, rather, a change in Sean's nap schedule. His morning and afternoon naps were combined into one midday nap, and Sean was once again content to go to bed at 8:00 PM.

Randy and Sharon also came to us with a problem caused by poor scheduling. Ten-month-old Gregory consistently woke at 4:30 AM, wanting to play. Sharon tried everything to get him to sleep longer. First she tried to make him stay in his crib and go back to sleep. Then she tried giving him some toys to play with in his crib, hoping that he would amuse himself while she and Randy slept. Nothing stopped his crying and everybody was tired.

An analysis of Gregory's sleep schedule showed that he slept soundly each night from 7:00 PM to 4:30 AM—a total of nine and a half hours. This was probably all the sleep that he needed. Sharon changed his bedtime to 9:00 PM and Gregory again slept nine and a half hours until 6:30 AM. This was a much better arrangement for the whole family.

Fifteen-month-old Heather was also driving her mother crazy with bad sleep habits. Heather was very inconsistent in her sleep routine. Some nights she would go to bed with no trouble, but other nights she would cry for hours. At times she would sleep straight through the night, but on other occasions she would wake up several times crying for her mother. Heather's problem also turned out to be a scheduling one. Her daily sleep schedule was too inconsistent for her to develop a predictable sleep pattern. Some days she would take a nap, other days she wouldn't. Sometimes she would be put to bed early, other times very late. It is important for a child to follow a consistent daily sleep/wake routine.

We all have an internal biological clock. This clock tells us when it's time to eat, sleep and wake. To keep this clock running on schedule, you need to set a daily rhythm that will cue your body with the sensations of hunger and sleepiness. After one week of a consistent daily schedule, Heather settled into a predictable and satisfactory sleep pattern.

What You Should Do: If you think you need to change your child's schedule, do it gradually. Judy changed Sean's bedtime from 7:00 PM to 9:00 PM in half-hour intervals each night. On the first night, she put him to bed at 7:30 PM; on the second night, at 8:00 PM; and so on until they reached the desired 9:00 PM bedtime.

Each child has his own individual sleep needs. No two children are ever exactly alike. To establish an appropriate schedule for your baby, you can't just ask your neighbor what time her children go to bed. You have to watch your own child. Note what time he wakes up and when he shows signs of tiredness, such as rubbing his eyes or acting fussy. How much sleep does he seem to need to wake up happy and refreshed?

Finding your baby's own natural sleep patterns is the key to success in ending sleep problems that stem from poor scheduling.

Environmental Stress

Kelly brought nine-month-old Steven to us because he had been waking up and crying one or two times every night for the last month. Kelly was at the end of her rope because, without sleep, she didn't have the energy to move her family into their new home. Before suggesting the Quick-Check Method, we advised Kelly to put up with the problem just until the move was completed and the family had settled back into its normal routine. As we suspected, once the stress of moving was over, so was Steven's sleep problem.

Research by R. F. Anders shows that night waking in infants can definitely be related to shifts and stresses in the environment. Babies are quick to tune in to family stress factors such as marital discord, job related difficulties, sickness in the family, divorce, unemployment, a death in the family or any other problem that causes tension.

What You Should Do: To ease the effects of environmental stress on your baby's sleep, you must first identify the problem. When did the crying start and what was going on in your household at that time? Once you have pinpointed the cause, try to eliminate it or cope better with it. If you can do that, and your baby's sleep problem is indeed caused by environmental stress, then you should see an improvement in your baby's sleep habits in one to two weeks. During this time be sure to give your child extra doses of attention and comfort during the day.

Temperament

1. Some infants, between the ages of six and twelve months, wake and cry out at night because they have what doctors call a

low sensory threshold. This means that, by nature, they are easily aroused by sounds, light and sudden movements. If you suspect your child has a low sensory threshold, observe his behavior during his waking hours. Does he excite easily? Is he easily startled by noise? Is he easily overstimulated by play activities? Does he have a low pain threshold? Does he use crying to relieve tension? If he does, he may be a night crier because of his temperament.

What You Should Do: The best way to help ease the night waking caused by a low sensory threshold is to reduce the external stimuli that may be bothering your child.

To Reduce Noise

- Try to keep your other family members quiet during naptime and sleeptime.
- Close the windows to deaden street noises.
- Use a white noise device in the baby's room. White noise is a constant and monotonous sound made by things such as an air conditioner, dehumidifier, low-powered vac- uum, rhythmic wave recordings, and between-channel radio static. These will help muffle external sounds.

To Reduce Light

- Use dark blinds or blackout curtains.

To Reduce Other Stimulators

- Try to keep a calm household environment when prepar- ing the baby for bed.

2. Pat used the Quick-Check Method with her two-year-old Billy because he had awakened crying several times every night since he was born. The method worked, in that Billy learned to put himself back to sleep each time he woke crying. But Pat was still worried because although she no longer had to get up with him all night long, he was still yelling out every few hours. We asked Pat to describe Billy's daytime personality. She was quick to reply, "Hyper!" Whether or not Billy was actually hyperactive from a medical viewpoint, he was a very restless and active little boy. That personality went with him to bed and also caused him to be a restless sleeper.

What You Should Do: If you think that your little one may be a restless sleeper simply because he is a restless child, then you must accept his personality the way it is at night. Although there is nothing you can do to stop it completely, like Pat, you can make the nighttime more bearable for yourself by using the Quick-Check Method to teach your child how to soothe himself back to sleep each time he wakes up crying.

You also can help him fall into a deeper sleep state by making sure he gets lots of fresh air and exercise during the day.

Constitutionally Poor Sleeper

Paula and Ed came to us looking for a solution to their two-year-old's sleep problem. They claimed that little Bobby "never slept." Although that wasn't quite true, it certainly seemed that way to his parents. Bobby didn't take any daytime naps, and he went to bed at 10:00 PM, and he woke at 2:00 AM every night.

He refused to go back to sleep and, even with the Quick-Check Method, he would cry persistently until morning.

After looking into every possible reason for this night waking, we found no answers. Bobby's parents had to accept the news that Bobby was one of the rare children who needs very little sleep.

What You Should Do: The only thing that Paula and Ed could do to make the situation more bearable was to move Bobby's bedtime up to 12:00 AM so they could use every minute of his sleep-time for their own sleep needs.

If you suspect that your child is one of these rare constitutionally poor sleepers, try charting his sleep needs for a few days. Note what time he gets up every day. Watch carefully for signs of tiredness. Don't even try to put him down for a nap. Just watch and see what happens. This is the only way you'll become aware of his individual sleep needs. Once you've identified what his sleep needs really are, then all you can do is work *with* them.

Medication

Sometimes a child's night waking may be caused or complicated by medication. The following is a list of drugs that most commonly affect sleep patterns.

Alcohol: It is not uncommon for desperate parents to spike their baby's nighttime bottle with some kind of alcohol. Although alcohol may cause a baby to fall asleep faster, it will also make him more restless and wakeful later in the night. Alcohol is never the solution to a sleeping problem.

Antibiotics: Many childhood illnesses are commonly treated with antibiotics. Some antibiotics cause excessive sleepiness and are also known to disrupt normal sleep patterns.

Antihistamines: This type of drug is commonly sold over the counter for the relief of cold and allergy symptoms, such as sinus congestion and itching, and for swelling. One of its side effects is drowsiness. You may think your child's sleep pattern has improved if he is taking medication containing this drug. Or your doctor might recommend the commonly used antihistamine Benadryl, or a major antihistamine sedative, such as phenobarbital, to help your baby sleep. Whether the drug affects your child's sleep as a side effect or as an intentional sleep treatment, the only positive consequence is that you might get a full night's sleep. Your child will still have a sleep problem that can be masked with drugs only for a short time.

Stimulants: Stimulants are often used to treat hyperactivity in children. However, drugs like Ritalin or Cylert may also be responsible for a child's disturbed sleep patterns.

You should also keep in mind that the stimulant caffeine, which may affect your child's sleep, is found in coffee, tea, cola and chocolate.

What You Should Do: Talk to your pediatrician. Ask him if any of your child's medications may be affecting his sleep. Perhaps he can recommend changes in the dosage or time of intake. There may be an alternative medication without the unwanted side effects. It may also help to switch from liquid form (which often contains sleep-disturbing additives) to pill form.

Or, if your doctor agrees, take your child off all medication to see what happens to the sleep problem. Once the sleep-disturbing drug is removed from your baby's system, he will be rid of the physical problem that woke him at night. However, if during that time of restless sleep he became accustomed to your night-time comforting, he may still cry for you during the night. Then the Quick-Check Method is needed to reestablish independent sleep habits.

Medical Problems

The Quick-Check Method is never an appropriate solution to night crying caused by medical problems. Chronic sleep problems often plague children who have central-nervous-system dysfunctions, such as hyperactivity, epilepsy, and cerebral palsy. These kinds of sleep disorders are beyond the scope of our sleep training method.

Occasionally sleep problems will develop because of common childhood medical problems or physical discomforts. The following is a list of problems that may keep your baby awake at night:

middle ear infection

teething pain

diaper rash

colic

nappy discomfort

food allergy

hypoglycemia

nappy rash

hunger

nasal congestion

sore throat

eczema

urinary tract infection

What You Should Do: Before using the Quick-Check Method, ask your doctor to rule out any medical problem that may be causing disruptive sleep patterns. Like the children on sleep-disturbing medication, however, these children who wake because of pain may want their parent's nighttime comfort even after the pain is gone. Then the Quick-Check Method is needed.

6

COPING WITH THE STRESS OF A NIGHT-CRYING BABY

Stress management and sleep training are not separate exercises. The Quick-Check Method has been built around the stress management techniques described in this chapter. Their inclusion in this program is a unique aspect of our approach to night waking. When you decide to help your baby break his poor sleep associations, you'll need a reserve of mental stamina to carry you through the night.

This chapter is designed to help you manage the stress of having a crying baby as well as the stress you may feel when you begin sleep training. Earlier in this book, we talked about the stress caused by the sound of a baby's cry, the stressful effect that a crying baby has on your family relationships and the stress caused by the constant disruption of your sleep cycle. Now it's time to learn how to deal with this problem.

Our stress management program is called the Three-Step

Stress Management Program. It is the same program offered to parents at our Crying Baby Clinic. A list of stress management tips is also included at the end of this chapter.

Three-Step Stress Management Program

Step 1. Understanding Stress

We believe that stress is the way our bodies respond when excited. The thing that excites us or produces the stress is called the stress trigger. The stress trigger may be physical (exhaustion, injury, extreme excitement), environmental (loud noises, noxious odors) or psychological (divorce, death of a family member, being fired), but it isn't always negative.

These triggers can range from an exciting baseball game to a nasty office memo, from a baby's cry to a totally engrossing murder mystery. The body's reaction, however, is the same regardless of what triggered the stress. The roots of the body's physical response go back to the days of primitive man. In the caveman era, the difference between bringing an animal home to eat and being eaten by the animal was man's ability to react quickly to danger. His body was able to prepare for fight or flight at a moments notice. To do this, his breathing became faster and shallower to bring more oxygen into his body quickly. His heartbeat increased to push that oxygen and increased blood sugar through the blood stream rapidly. And the blood flow was redirected from the internal organs and the surface of the body to the deep muscles, which needed more energy to prepare for the fight.

Those people who had quick stress-response systems survived and became our ancestors. The problem is that our ancestors' stress response, which was designed to promote the physical activity of running away or fighting, is no longer appropriate for us. This physical response to stress may have helped our ancestors to survive, but it's killing us.

Today's parents no longer need extra oxygen directed to their deep muscles when they hear their baby cry, yet it still happens. Our body prepares us to fight, but most often we have no foe. So what happens? Our heart beats rapidly, our blood pressure is elevated, our muscles tighten, and after a while our body begins to wear down. We develop physical illnesses such as ulcers, headaches, heart palpitations, backaches, rashes, colitis, allergies, asthma, heart disease, diabetes, and (as found in the latest research) even cancer.

To deal with the stress of raising a crying baby, you must first recognize the way your body reacts to this stress, and then give yourself permission to treat it. If you don't, you will eventually break down physically.

When you begin managing your stress, try to put your problems into the proper perspective. We know that a crying baby can overwhelm the senses. He can monopolize your thoughts and actions twenty-four hours a day, and he can cause you more stress than you've ever felt before. So, before doing any sleep training with your baby, take a deep breath and remind yourself that this baby is only little for a relatively short period of time. And remember that night crying is a common child rearing problem that *can* be solved.

When Barbara brought seventeen-month-old Jerry to our clinic, she was physically and emotionally distraught. Recalling that first day, Barbara later told us, "The single most important thing that reduced my stress was just knowing that you would give me a structured and time-limited program that could teach my child how to sleep through the night." Like Barbara, most parents find that just knowing they can do something changes their despair into hope. This is the kind of attitude change that will also help you to practice stress management. Just remembering that stress is a biological phenomenon that happens to everyone is the first step.

Knowing stress is a part of everyone's life should also make it easier for you to admit openly that your night-waking baby is causing you to feel a lot of anxiety. This is nothing to be ashamed of or embarrassed about. Although society tells us to admire the nurse on the battlefield and the capable, high-pressured business person, these kinds of people are not really immune to stress. Either they are paying the price in physical ailments, or they have learned to manage it. No one is completely able to avoid it. Therefore management of stress, not its elimination, is the key.

Research fully supports what you already know: parenting is an extremely stressful occupation at its best. But research also shows that people in high-demand positions with little or no control over their situation are the ones who most often develop heart disease. Parenting a crying baby without being able to control the problem, then, must obviously cause excessive amounts of stress. It is important for you to believe that stress is not an abnormality in your life. When you try to deny or ignore it, it becomes impossible to treat. You must give yourself permission to see stress as just one of the many behaviors that your body exhibits. Then you can learn strategies that will let you control your biological reactions to this stress.

Step 2. Measuring and Eliminating Unnecessary Stress Triggers

Are you carrying around a lot of tension right now? Take this stress test and find out:

Stress Test

On a separate piece of paper, answer *true* or *false* to each of the following questions:

1. I often find myself daydreaming about other people who live a better life than I do.

2. I feel that I am more tense than other people my age and sex.

3. Sometimes my hands and feet get very cold, and I can't hold cold drinks at parties.

4. I always seem to be tired, and I can't get myself motivated to do things.

5. I never seem to have enough time to do the things that I am supposed to do.

6. I often find it hard to concentrate.

7. I have had trouble with my stomach (gassiness, ulcers, etc.) or with diarrhea and/or constipation.

8. My doctor has told me that I have high blood pressure.

9. I always seem to be keyed up.

10. I sweat a lot without overexerting myself.

11. It seems that I get angry at the slightest things.

12. Sometimes I have difficulty breathing, and I feel as if I can't get enough air.

Total *True* answers.

The more true answers you have, the more you can profit from stress management training. Even one or two true answers indicate you can benefit from practicing stress relief exercises.

Now use the Stress-Degree (SD) Ladder below to learn how to measure your stress response. Zero (0) represents complete relaxation and 100 represents complete panic—the worst possible state of terror that you can imagine. All the points in between represent different degrees or amounts of stress. When you feel more than 50 SD's, you are experiencing the effects of a significant stress trigger. Take a minute and fill in the blanks. This will make you comfortable with using SD's to measure your tension.

This Stress-Degree Ladder will help you think about different situations or things that trigger stress. Then when your baby starts his night-crying routine, you'll be able to judge how much stress you're experiencing by comparing your body's response to the ones listed on this ladder.

The Stress-Degree Scale in Appendix B will help you find hidden stress triggers. We know that a great deal of your stress comes from being the parent of a crying baby, but very often

Stress-Degree Ladder

Feelings Example		Stress Degrees
Completely relaxed	_____	0
	_____	10
Comfortable	_____	20
	_____	30
	_____	40
Moderately tense	_____	50
	_____	60
	_____	70
Uncomfortably tense	_____	80
	_____	90
Terror	_____	100

there are many other stress triggers present in your life at the same time. The Stress-Degree Scale will help you pinpoint them. Sharon, for example, came to us looking for help with her crying baby. It was obvious she was feeling a great deal of stress. But it wasn't until she began to record and measure her feelings of stress on the Stress-Degree Scale that another stress trigger became very apparent.

Sharon dreaded naptime. Her baby always seemed particularly fussy and difficult when he was tired. When all was finally quiet, Sharon would hold her breath and tiptoe around the house. Then the phone would ring. Every day at the same time Sharon's mum would call to chat. Sharon's heart would pound as she ran to the phone, praying it wouldn't wake the baby. She believed all her stress came from her crying baby, but just the thought of the phone disturbing his sleep was enough to raise her SD's to over 50. Once Sharon realized this phone call was a strong stress trigger, she was quickly able to change the situation. She learned to assert herself and told her mum to call at another time. We then instructed Sharon to take the phone off the hook during naptime so no one else would wake the baby.

Use the Stress-Degree Scale in appendix B to record exactly when your SD's go over 50. This will bring to light hidden stressors that may surprise you. Sharon's Stress-Degree Scale looked like this.

Stress Degrees

Record Tension Level Hourly or When It Elevates or Decreases Suddenly

Highest	Morning	Afternoon	Evening	Early Morning
100				
90				
80		X		
70		X	X	
60				
50				
40				
30				
20				
10				
0				
Lowest	7 8 9 10 11	12 1 2 3 4 5	6 7 8 9 10 11	12 1 2 3 4 5

It is also true that everyone fluctuates in their stress responses. Even your response to your baby's cry varies. If the baby starts to cry at 10 o'clock in the morning after you've had a few quiet hours alone, your SD's will be different than if he cries at 5:00 PM while his sibling is also acting up and you're trying to make dinner. Your response will be different again if you've been up all night nursing the fever of your older child when your night crier begins his routine.

The most efficient form of stress management involves measuring SD's, finding unknown stress triggers, and then eliminating them. But it's impossible for us to predict your stress triggers. Just remember that anything can be a stress trigger. Some, like a baby's cry, cannot be totally eliminated, but you can learn how to change your response to them. For example,

Record Below any Experience of Tension Above 50

	Antecedent (what happened just before)	Behavior (your experience of tension)	Consequence (what happened afterward)
1	I brought the baby into her room for her nap. She screamed.	My heart skipped a beat.	I patted her back until she fell asleep.
2	The house was finally quiet. The baby was asleep. The phone rang.	My mind began racing.	I ran to the phone and yelled at my mother.
3	I brought the baby into her bedroom for bedtime. She screamed.	I cried and felt my stomach drop.	I took her back to the living room.
4			

how you interpret the meaning of your baby's cry can cause it to be stressful or not. If you feel the cry means danger or pain, it will always be stressful. If you hear the cry as a protest, you'll probably be able to ignore it and not feel stressed. Once you begin to measure your stress and find the triggers you find troublesome, you will be able to eliminate or modify them.

Then you can feel mentally strong when you begin the Quick-Check Method.

Step 3. Stress Management Techniques

A number of techniques have been found to reduce stress. Some of these focus on modifying your response to certain triggers, like Sharon's need to be more assertive. Others concentrate on changing your body's response to stress by relaxing your muscles or breathing deeply. We are going to give you a general survey of different procedures. Although each is given only a brief presentation, you will find sources of more detailed information listed in the bibliography at the back of the book.

Noise Abatement: As we mentioned in chapter 3, just the sound of a baby's cry produces stress. Noise abatement simply means reducing the volume and intensity of the noise. You can try the following methods while using the Quick-Check Method:

1. Move to another part of the house. Invite any family member who is also having trouble with the noise to go with you. You can even spend the night in another room further away from the baby. The objective is to reduce the volume. Remember, this is only temporary and it will be worth the effort when it's over.

2. Wear earmuffs, earphones or earplugs.

3. Turn on the stereo or television.

4. Take a shower, or just sit in the bathroom with the water running.

5. Blow-dry your hair.

6. Run the vacuum. (Don't use it—you're trying to save your energy. Just turn it on.)

The noise that helps you muffle the sound of your baby's crying will not keep him awake any more than your tiptoeing around will help him fall asleep (as you probably already know). So turn up the noise and turn your attention away from the sound of crying.

Time Management: Time is a fixed commodity, and there's nothing we can do to expand it. As parents, you probably find yourself rushing from one frantic activity to another. But if a hurried schedule leaves you irritable and exhausted, then you're managing your time poorly. The sound of your baby's night cries causes you enough stress; you don't need the pressure of too little time added to that load. So while you're working with our Quick-Check Method, try to eliminate another stress trigger with proper time management.

Time management requires you to establish priorities for the activities in your life. To do that, list all your daily activities. List everything you do that takes up your time, from going to the office to cleaning the kitchen. Then rank each activity in priority order, with *1* being the highest (I can't live without it) activity, and *3* being the lowest. We suggest that, prior to sleep training, you should do away with 50 percent of your number *3* activities if you have one child. If you have two or more children, eliminate all of your number *3*'s. If, for example, reading junk mail is a *3* priority, don't open one piece of it during the sleep training period. Promise yourself not to take the time to read through things you didn't even ask to have delivered to your house—not now while your stress load is so high.

Also, if you find yourself complaining about the poor quality of television programming while you sit glued to the screen, you're practicing poor time management. Many overworked parents spend their prime time on the low-priority activity of watching TV. Don't be one of them. Spend your prime-time hours on top priorities.

Another way to improve your time schedule is to make use of the other people in your household. Let someone else do the low-priority tasks. Include everyone who is available to help—your spouse, siblings, children, friends and neighbors. You can't do everything you used to do before the baby, so delegate tasks as often as possible. Use the section on assertiveness training to help you.

Let someone else take charge of cleaning the house for a while. So what if your five-year-old doesn't dust as well as you do? Right now you're working to eliminate external stress triggers. It doesn't matter if your house isn't as clean as usual. If you're worrying that someone will drop by and be shocked by the mess, hang the sign on page 105 on your front door.

Because a strong state of mental health is imperative during this period, always make sure at least one high-priority activity on your daily schedule allows time just for *you*—even if it's just to complete one page of a novel you've been anxious to read. It is impossible to deal with your baby's night crying when you're in tears from uncertainty and exhaustion. If you can establish a reserve of stamina within yourself, you'll have more patience to

---

NOTICE

We are sleep training (baby's name).

For the next week

the following can be expected:

1. crying at night
2. dishes in the sink
3. a messy house
4. short-tempered parents

Enter only if you have support to give.

---

deal with your night crier in the wee hours of the morning.

Prior to sleep training, try to get all necessary chores done (paying monthly bills, etc.). Shop for two weeks, precook and freeze meals, and have your two-week menu prepared. When sleep training begins, you'll have more time for rest and relaxation during the day.

Thought Control: When your baby cries at night, listen to what you say to yourself. Do you remind yourself how unfair it is that you have to be up with this child when none of your friends have this problem with their children? Do you tell yourself how inadequate you must be? Do you dwell on your exhaustion and curse your baby for stealing your sleep? If this sounds like the way you talk to yourself, then your own thoughts are making it harder for you to bear the stress of your crying baby. The technique of thought control eliminates this internal source of stress by forcing you to think positively.

If you find yourself wrapped up in negative thoughts when

your baby won't go to sleep, stop yourself and immediately construct a rational alternative. Argue for the positive side as if you were an attorney for the defense in a court of law. State to yourself: "This situation has nothing to do with me. Indeed, this behavior is more likely the product of improper learning that can be corrected. I'm involved in a program that is designed to teach a new behavior and I have every reason to believe that the program is going to be effective." Further defend yourself by asking: "Why should I, of all parents, fail in this sleep training attempt?" Challenge your fears. Argue against them. Write down rational alternatives. Use this line of defense whenever you find yourself falling back into the same pattern of negative thoughts.

Teaching your baby to sleep is not always an easy process. When you find yourself saying something negative like, "This isn't going to work" (and you will say that), challenge it, and replace it with a positive thought. Recognize that control of your internal language is as important as your control of external factors.

The basis of thought control as a method of stress management is simple: When you talk to yourself, say something positive.

Assertiveness Training: Can you assert yourself? The ability to do this is involved in almost every aspect of sleep training and stress management. Many parents feel guilty and anxious when trying to use assertive behavior. This is unfortunate because assertive behavior is simply a way of expressing your feelings and practicing basic human rights. It allows you to see yourself as being as important as everyone else.

Mary was the parent of a fifteen-month-old night crier. We told her that she couldn't begin the Quick-Check Method until she learned to assert herself. Her husband, Bill, felt it was her responsibility to take care of their child. He was often angry with her for not being able to keep the baby quiet at night so he could get a good night's sleep. "After all," he reasoned, "when I'm at work, you can take a nap. You have nothing to do all day anyway."

Unlike many couples who come to our Crying Baby Clinic, Mary had come alone. Not only did Bill believe it was totally her responsibility to find a solution to the night crying, but so did Mary! We told her that she could not find a solution to her baby's problem until she was ready to stand up and ask for her husband's support.

We started our work with Mary by having her participate in an Angry Assertiveness-Training Exercise. This exercise has four steps:

1. Express how you feel right now.

2. Tell the other person what he does that upsets you.

3. Tell the person the effect of that behavior on you.

4. Tell the person how he can change his behavior in order for you to feel differently.

Mary's paper read:

1. I feel angry, depressed and dumped on.

2. You make me responsible for keeping the house quiet so you can get a good night's sleep.

3. You make me feel unimportant and humiliated.

4. If you would share responsibility for sleep training our baby by alternating the quick checks, I would feel more like a wife and less like a servant.

We sent Mary home to share these feelings with her husband. A few days later, she and Bill came back to us. They were now both ready to begin the Quick-Check Method.

Assertive behavior also will be necessary if you live in an apartment. Inform your neighbors that you will be sleep training your son or daughter and that they may hear crying at night. Assert yourself by hanging up the door sign mentioned in the section on time management. You can't succeed at sleep training if you're too concerned about everyone else's opinion. These are stress triggers that you can do without. Like Mary, you need to be assertive and look to the people who care about you for support.

If you need more guidance to feel comfortable about asserting yourself, assertiveness-training programs are commercially available. You can also look for books in the library on the subject as these are often full of very good ideas.

Deep Breathing: Since the body needs oxygen to fuel its stress response, you can reduce or short circuit the stress you feel by regaining control of your breathing. Athletes will often do this just before the race begins or as they are about to get up to bat.

· To stop the rapid breathing accompanying a stress response: Put your hand on your stomach.

· Take a deep breath from the bottom of your stomach. Feel it fill you with warm air. Feel your hand rise with your stomach muscles.
· Breathe in as you silently count to five.
· Let the air go. Don't push it out. Let it go gently to the count of five.
· When you let out the air, smile.
· Do this sequence two times in a row.
· Then breathe regularly (rhythmically and comfortably).
· Deep breathe again after you have let a minute or two go by.
· Repeat this deep-breathing/regular-breathing cycle two or three times, or as often as needed, until you find your breathing has returned to a natural and comfortable pace.

We have recommended that you smile when you exhale because it's a natural mood elevator. While you're smiling, it's difficult to be stressed. Try this experiment: think nasty thoughts while you're smiling. Don't just say nasty words, but actually think and feel nasty thoughts while you're smiling. Isn't it hard? That's why you can help your body to ease its tension if you smile when you exhale.

Deep breathing is a strategy you can use anywhere. No one around needs to know you're practicing a stress reduction technique. It's a technique you can engage in whenever you feel yourself stressed. When your baby cries, immediately begin deep breathing. Without changing your thoughts or actions, deep breathing will change your body's reaction to stress.

Guided Imagery: Because we all daydream and nightdream, we already know we have an internal world that we can experience in both positive and negative ways. Guided imagery requires you go to that inner world and construct a place where you'll feel safe and relaxed whenever you imagine yourself being there.

To better understand how guided imagery works in a postive way, let's first take a look at how a negative image can produce its own stress:

· Using the technique described on pages 98–99, record the level of your SD's right now.
· Read through this passage:

It is 2:00 AM. You've just put your night crier back to bed for the second time. He's been especially cranky all week, and he has disturbed everyone's sleep for the last five nights. You're especially bothered by his night crying now, because earlier in the day your next-door neighbor asked if you could please do something to stop the baby from crying so much at night. You're also hoping this won't be another bad night because your mother-in-law arrived unannounced for an overnight visit, and your husband needs a good night's sleep to be alert for an important early-morning meeting. Just as you lay your head back down on the pillow, the crying starts again. Your husband heaves a loud sigh of disgust, and your mother-in-law is out in the hall asking, "What's the matter with the baby?" Your hands are shaking with rage, and your heart is pounding, as tears begin to cloud your vision. Your only thought is, "I just can't stand another minute of that crying!"

· Now, close your eyes and imagine all of that happening to you.

Open your eyes and record your SD's now.

Most people report an increase in SD's after just imagining such a scene. It is true that the internal experience alone—the image—can produce a stress response.

Since a negative image can produce stress so easily, it's only logical that a positive image can reduce it. The core belief of the guided imagery approach is that imagining a positive experience can stop, interrupt or prevent a stress reaction.

To do this, create a positive image in your mind that represents a safe and relaxing environment. Practice visiting it over and over again. Then when you are stressed, you can go there just briefly and benefit from the relaxed feeling it gives you.

For example, this is an image that we find soothing:

I am stretched out on the beach at Long Beach Island, New Jersey. The sun is warm on my body. When it gets too strong, I have an umbrella for protection. I feel the warmth of the sand in my fingertips. I see the calm ocean touching the shore. I can smell the salt of the ocean, and I can taste the sea air. On my beach there's just the right number of people—I'm not crowded or lonely. On my beach there are no sand crabs or flies. I feel just wonderful. It's an ideal place that I can visit with all my senses anytime I want. Even when I'm in the middle of a crowd with my eyes wide open, I can go to my beach. I can even listen to a baby cry for twenty minutes and still go there to enjoy the comfort it gives me.

This safe place happens to be a beach—yours can be anywhere. It can be in your family room by the fireplace, the woods by a stream, the park down the street. It can be anywhere, but there are certain things you should keep in mind:

- If you start to create your safe place and you find anything wrong (any elevation in SD's), take out the negative image. The possibilities of a location are unlimited, so find an area that is *perfect*.
- Make the place real. When you're stressed, you won't be able to relate fully to an alien planet.
- Involve all of your senses. Make sure all the smells, and the things you touch, taste, hear and see in this environment are pleasing to you.
- The more you practice increasing the quality of your image, the more you can rely on it when you're stressed. It will become an overpracticed response.

This technique can be used in even the most stressful situations. You might even try to incorporate the sound of your baby's cry into your scene. Let the repetitive wails be the waves on the surf, or the squealing of excited children at the amusement park. Or close down the sound completely by making some other sound in your image more intense. You can even concentrate on your internal image to block out external sounds. You were practicing this skill every time someone said to you, "Didn't you hear me calling you?" And you answered, "No, I was thinking about something." People who are engrossed in deep thought, a book or a TV show may honestly not hear anything else around them. You can use this same deep-thought idea to block out the sound of your night crier. Guided imagery will ease the wear of stress by stopping your body's stress reaction.

Give it a try. Close your eyes and find that place inside of you that is peaceful and safe.

Progressive Muscle Relaxation: The goal of Progressive Muscle Relaxation is to teach you how to recognize muscle tension and then how to relax the muscles. In stressful situations many people describe the way they feel as being "tied up in knots." Because of the way our muscles react to stress, this is actually true. Progressive Muscle Relaxation will enable you to untie those knots. Then, when you feel stress in stomach cramps, headaches, stiff neck muscles, etc., you can make those muscles relax and ease the effects of stress on your body. Although we all have the ability to relax our muscles, that ability is not something we consciously use. By practicing Progressive Muscle Relaxation, you will learn what it feels like when stress begins to manifest itself in muscle tension. Then when your muscles do begin to tense, you will be able to identify the problem area and stop the stress attack.

To begin, tense and relax the various muscle groups listed on page 114. Maintain that tension for fifteen seconds so you have time to feel how whole parts of your body are involved in tension. When you have a muscle group tensed, let your mind's eye experience that part of your body. If you're tensing your arm, for example, press your forearm down against the table. Feel where the tension goes out through your fingertips, up onto your shoulders, right into your neck—then relax. Feel the experience of letting go—of consciously relaxing your muscles.

There is no magic in this list of muscle groups. Pick ones that make sense for you and practice until you're well acquainted with the feeling of tension in each one. Then give the method a chance to relieve the stress you feel in your life. The next time your night crier gets you up at 2:00 AM, try this technique when you get back into bed. Let your mind's eye go through your body to ascertain the location of the tension. For many people it's commonly in the lower back, neck or shoulders; for others it's in and around the forehead or the jaw area. When you've found your tense area, use the skill of Progressive Muscle Relaxation to ease the muscles that have become a stress trigger for you.

Repeat the following exercise three times with these muscle groups:

1. right hand   make a fist
    right forearm   press down
2. left hand   make a fist
    left forearm   press down
3. shoulders   shrug
4. neck   lean your head back and
                            roll it from side to side

5. head:
    jaw   bite down lightly
    tongue   press on the roof of your
                            mouth
    eyes   squint
    forehead   frown and raise your
                            brows
6. abdomen   tighten your stomach as if
                            someone were going to
                            hit you
7. back   arch slightly
8. right leg   press down on the floor
    left leg   press down on the floor
9. toes   curl under

If you have medical complications which would make it impossible for you to do this, consult your physician or see a professional stress management specialist for guidance.

Autogenic Training: Autogenic training is based on self-generated statements. Its goal is to make you concentrate on a statement that you say to yourself over and over again until you have blocked out the external stress trigger.

Give this example a try: In your mind's eye focus on your right arm and right hand. Try to experience them completely by taking a journey through them. Feel how they touch the chair. Feel your arm's hair touch the upholstery, your ring touch your finger, your shirt lie on your shoulder. When you are completely aware of your arm and hand, repeat a relaxing phrase over and over again. Try something like:

"My right arm is heavy and warm. The warmth is flowing into my hand." Or, "My right arm is light and cool. It feels like it's floating." (Or whatever statement describes how you feel when you are relaxed.) Then stop and take a look at your hand and arm, and describe to yourself how they feel. Do they feel warm and heavy? Light? What does the sensation of relaxation feel like?

This process, like Progressive Muscle Relaxation, will take your mind away from your baby's cries and place all your powers of concentration on something else. You can practice Autogenic Training with whatever part of your body feels tense. You can do this along with Progressive Muscle Relaxation or in place of it. When the sound of your baby's cry raises your SD's over 50, you may have to try a variety of relaxation exercises until you find the one that will work at that moment. Sometimes you may find it hard to go to your safe place or to concentrate on muscle relaxation. You might find it easier to repeat your relaxing phrase. Only you can decide what will work best.

Twenty Stress Management Tips

1. Eliminate as many unnecessary stress triggers as possible. (Take the phone off the hook during naptime.)

2. Smile as often as you can.

3. Manage time by cutting out low-priority tasks. (Wash the dishes only once a day.)

4. Hang up note cards around the house that remind you to breathe deeply and to experience some of your guided images.

5. Share household responsibilities with as many people as possible. (Hire a neighborhood teenager to help you out.)

6. Hang up positive-thought phrases. (I can do it!)

7. Provide yourself with some personally rewarding activities during prime time. (Guarantee yourself at least fifteen minutes after dinner.)

8. Exercise to keep your body in shape. Remember, the stress response was originally designed for physical activity so

your ability to rebound depends on your general health and conditioning.

9. Share your intent to begin sleep training with as many friends and relatives as possible. This will eliminate surprises.

10. Reduce your intake of caffeinated drinks and food (coffee, tea, cola and chocolate). They are powerful stimulants that your stressed body doesn't need right now.

11. Develop a personal support network of people. When the going gets tough, call them. Teach them to be your cheerleaders.

12. Learn how to say "No" without guilt.

13. Decide on a realistic but special reward for you and your family that will motivate you to complete the program successfully. Post it everywhere and think of it when you feel yourself getting upset. (Take a special trip.)

14. Catch yourself trying to interpret your child's crying at night. Just treat it as a learned behavior.

15. Catch yourself making negative self-statements and replace them with positive self-statements.

16. Take one day at a time.

17. Give yourself the right to make mistakes.

18. Keep track of your stress degrees and try to maintain a positive internal and external environment.

19. Use noise abatement techniques to reduce the sound of crying.

20. Cut down on your smoking. Nicotine aggravates the body's phsyical response to stress.

7

GOOD LUCK AND SWEET DREAMS

We end this book as we began it: You are not alone. You and your baby have a problem that is quite common. So don't feel guilty about your child's sleep difficulty. We have found that parents who come to our clinic are not "bad" or "inadequate"; they simply have been ineffective because they lack knowledge. This guide should resolve this information deficiency and help you end your child's night-crying habit.

If, after reading this book, you still are uncertain or confused about what is causing your child's sleep disorder or how to stop it, don't hesitate to consult a pediatrician.

Appendix A: Quick-Check Chart

	Night #1 Quick-Check Time	Night #2 Quick-Check Time	Night #3 Quick-Check Time	Night #4 Quick-Check Time	Night #5 Quick-Check Time	Night #6 Quick-Check Time	Night #7 Quick-Check Time
Start of Crying Time							
Check #1							
Check #2							
Check #3							
Check #4							
Check #5							
Check #6							
Check #7							
Sleeptime							
Total Crying Time							

	Night #1	Night #2	Night #3	Night #4	Night #5	Night #6	Night #7
	Quick-Check Time	Quick-Check Time	Quick-Check Time	Quick-Check Time	Quick-Check Time	Quick-Check Time	Quick-Check Time
Wake-up #1							
Check #1							
Check #2							
Check #3							
Check #4							
Check #5							
Check #6							
Check #7							
Sleeptime							
Total Crying Time							

	Night #1	Night #2	Night #3	Night #4	Night #5	Night #6	Night #7
	Quick-Check Time	Quick-Check Time	Quick-Check Time	Quick-Check Time	Quick-Check Time	Quick-Check Time	Quick-Check Time
Wake-up #2							
Check #1							
Check #2							
Check #3							
Check #4							
Check #5							
Check #6							
Check #7							
Sleeptime							
Total Crying Time							

Appendix A: Quick-Check Chart

	Night #1	Night #2	Night #3	Night #4	Night #5	Night #6	Night #7
	Quick-Check Time	*Quick-Check Time*	*Quick-Check Time*	*Quick-Check Time*	*Quick-Check Time*	*Quick-Check Time*	*Quick-Check Time*
Start of Crying Time							
Check #1							
Check #2							
Check #3							
Check #4							
Check #5							
Check #6							
Check #7							
Sleeptime							
Total Crying Time							

	Night #1	Night #2	Night #3	Night #4	Night #5	Night #6	Night #7
	Quick-Check Time	Quick-Check Time	Quick-Check Time	Quick-Check Time	Quick-Check Time	Quick-Check Time	Quick-Check Time
Wake-up #1							
Check #1							
Check #2							
Check #3							
Check #4							
Check #5							
Check #6							
Check #7							
Sleeptime							
Total Crying Time							

	Night #1 Quick-Check Time	Night #2 Quick-Check Time	Night #3 Quick-Check Time	Night #4 Quick-Check Time	Night #5 Quick-Check Time	Night #6 Quick-Check Time	Night #7 Quick-Check Time
Wake-up #2							
Check #1							
Check #2							
Check #3							
Check #4							
Check #5							
Check #6							
Check #7							
Sleeptime							
Total Crying Time							

126

Appendix A: Quick-Check Chart

	Night #1	Night #2	Night #3	Night #4	Night #5	Night #6	Night #7
	Quick-Check Time	Quick-Check Time	Quick-Check Time	Quick-Check Time	Quick-Check Time	Quick-Check Time	Quick-Check Time
Start of Crying Time							
Check #1							
Check #2							
Check #3							
Check #4							
Check #5							
Check #6							
Check #7							
Sleeptime							
Total Crying Time							

	Night #1	Night #2	Night #3	Night #4	Night #5	Night #6	Night #7
	Quick-Check Time	Quick-Check Time	Quick-Check Time	Quick-Check Time	Quick-Check Time	Quick-Check Time	Quick-Check Time
Wake-up #1							
Check #1							
Check #2							
Check #3							
Check #4							
Check #5							
Check #6							
Check #7							
Sleeptime							
Total Crying Time							

	Night #1	Night #2	Night #3	Night #4	Night #5	Night #6	Night #7
	Quick-Check Time	Quick-Check Time	Quick-Check Time	Quick-Check Time	Quick-Check Time	Quick-Check Time	Quick-Check Time
Wake-up #2							
Check #1							
Check #2							
Check #3							
Check #4							
Check #5							
Check #6							
Check #7							
Sleeptime							
Total Crying Time							

Appendix B: Stress-Degree Scale
Stress Degrees

Record Tension Level Hourly or When It Elevates or Decreases Suddenly

Highest	Morning	Afternoon	Evening	Early Morning
100				
90				
80				
70				
60				
50				
40				
30				
20				
10				
0				
Lowest	7 8 9 10 11 12	1 2 3 4 5 6	7 8 9 10 11 12	1 2 3 4 5 6

Record Below any Experience of Tension Above 50 SD's

	Antecedent (what happened just before)	Behavior (your experience of tension)	Consequence (what happened afterward)
1			
2			
3			
4			

Appendix B: Stress-Degree Scale
Stress Degrees

Record Tension Level Hourly or When It Elevates or Decreases Suddenly

Highest	Morning	Afternoon	Evening	Early Morning
100				
90				
80				
70				
60				
50				
40				
30				
20				
10				
0				

Lowest   7 8 9 10 11 12 1 2 3 4 5 6 7 8 9 10 11 12 1 2 3 4 5 6

Record Below any Experience of Tension Above 50 SD's

	Antecedent (what happened just before)	Behavior (your experience of tension)	Consequence (what happened afterward)
1			
2			
3			
4			

Appendix B: Stress-Degree Scale
Stress Degrees

Record Tension Level Hourly or When It Elevates or Decreases Suddenly

Highest	Morning	Afternoon	Evening	Early Morning
100				
90				
80				
70				
60				
50				
40				
30				
20				
10				
0				
Lowest	7 8 9 10 11 12	1 2 3 4 5 6	7 8 9 10 11 12	1 2 3 4 5 6

Record Below any Experience of Tension Above 50

	Antecedent (what happened just before)	Behavior (your experience of tension)	Consequence (what happened afterward)
1			
2			
3			
4			

133

BIBLIOGRAPHY

Benson, Herbert, *The Relaxation Response* (Fount, 1977)

Ferber, Richard, *Solve Your Child's Sleep Problems* (Dorling Kindersley, 1986)

Green, C., *Toddler Taming* (Century, 1984)

Haslam, David, *Sleepless Children: A Handbook for Parents* (Futura, 1985)

Jacobson, Edmund, *You Must Relax* (Unwin, 1980)

Lakein, Alan, *How to Get Control of Your Time and Your Life* (Gower, 1985)

Smith, Manuel, *When I Say No, I Feel Guilty* (Bantam, 1976)

Index

T

U

Of further interest . . .

TOILET-TRAINING & BED-WETTING

A Practical Guide For Today's Parents

Heather Welford

Learning about bowel and bladder control is a normal part of a child's development that we, as parents, merely help them to achieve. It shouldn't be a problem, and it shouldn't be a question of you imposing your will on your child's.

So why *is* it a problem? Why should a parent want to seek the advice of their doctor, health visitor, neighbour, friend or magazine because of the anxiety that is being caused? Why *do* so many parents feel that it has gone wrong?

This book will answer some of the worries that arise when lack of information and lack of confidence combine. However, it is up to the parents to decide on the best method of toilet-training — and this decision should be based on what *you* feel is right for you and your child.

Heather Welford is the mother of three children. She also has many years' experience of offering advice to others through her work on *Parents* magazine.

CRYING FOR HELP

How to cure your child of colic

Carol Young

- Types, causes of and remedies for colic
- Hints to help babies to sleep
- Breast feeding and colic
- Soothing the unsettled baby

About thirty per cent of all babies born suffer from acute attacks of abdominal pain which begin shortly after birth and usually continue until the baby is about three months old.

Carol Young outlines the symptoms and types of colic, exposing the fallacies and giving ways of overcoming the problems, including herbal remedies, mineral and vitamin supplements and the use of homoeopathy.

An invaluable source of help and comfort to distressed parents with a crying child.